W9-AES-550

Faculty Leadership:
A Reflective Practice Guide for
Community College Faculty

Sue Wells MA ECE RT

Lisa McCaie B. Ed ECE RT

Megan Barker MA

Marilyn Herie PhD RSW

© 2018 Sue Wells, Lisa McCaie, Megan Barker & Marilyn Herie

All Rights Reserved.

No part of this publication may be reproduced, stored in a retrieval system, or transmitted, in any form or by any means, electronic, mechanical, photocopying, recording, or otherwise, without the written permission of the author.

This edition published by
Dog Ear Publishing
4011 Vincennes Road
Indianapolis, IN 46268

www.dogearpublishing.net

ISBN: 978-145756-143-6
This book is printed on acid-free paper.

Contributors

The authors would like to gratefully acknowledge the following individuals for contribution of their tools for reflection and/or the piloting of select tools within the guide and allowing us to share their personal reflections.

Helen Anderson , Christine Cox, Marah Echavez, Thomas Nault, Paola Ostinelli, Jenny Quianzon, Yasmin Razack

Inspiration

This manual was inspired by Wells and Herie, *Academic Leadership: A Reflective Practice Guide for Community College Chairs (2017)*. Some of the content found within this guide has been adapted from that source.

Acknowledgements

The authors would like to gratefully acknowledge the following Centennial College faculty members for their review and feedback of earlier drafts of this manuscript.

- Jackie Bishop
- Pauline Camuti Cull
- Lorne Hilts
- Carol Preston

We would also like to express our appreciation to Marisa ChinYan and Olga Babenko for their tireless assistance in coordinating and supporting the development of this resource.

Finally, we extend our gratitude to Ann Buller, President and CEO of Centennial College, for her visionary and inspirational leadership.

Cover Design: Bruce Williams   Cover Photo: Marilyn Herie

The Reflective Practice Manual is thoughtful, thought-provoking, creative and enormously helpful. The content challenged my understanding of reflective practice and I recommend this manual as required reading for all faculty.
Carol Preston,
Professor, School of Engineering Technology and Applied Science

The guided exercises provide focus and intention to my teaching practice. The added component of peer collaboration offers greater depth and meaning to the process of reflective practice.
Pauline Camuti-Cull, *BA, RECE, CS,*
Professor, Early Childhood Education

This manual offers a practical and engaging resource for new and seasoned college faculty. As an educator it is important to reflect on our teaching practice in meaningful ways. The rich array of tools and resources foster continued growth and professional development.
Lorne Hilts, *RFM, RLS,*
Professor, Recreation and Leisure Services

Table of Contents

Table of Contents

Introduction

"The way of teaching demands a long journey that does not have any easily identifiable destination. It is a journey that I believe must include a backward step into the self and it is a journey that is its own destination."

- Robert Tremmel

Teaching sounds simple – it is familiar and inherent in many aspects of our lives. We have all taught someone something – to make a recipe, tie a shoe, or operate a drill. Despite how deeply ingrained teaching is in our lives, teaching is an art, requiring those who practice it to become masters of their craft. Teachers have the power to impart wisdom, inspire learners, and support students in learning both within and beyond face-to-face and online classrooms.

Learning is most effective when facilitated through the principles and applications of evidence-based and innovative adult learning models and approaches. Adult learning is one component of a larger and more extended learning process, and today's workforce requires learners to go beyond mastering competencies. Lifelong learning demands capabilities (learning how to learn) as our rapidly-changing workforce advances and expands competency needs (Frenk et al., 2010). To meet the demands of this dynamic learning environment, your most important role as a college faculty member is to offer your students a transformative learning experience of the highest caliber.

The practice of teaching within the college context is far from simple. Learners come to your classroom with a wide range of learning abilities and styles, cultural backgrounds, personal experiences, and unique characteristics. As a faculty member, you must consider and meet the needs of a diverse student body through culturally-responsive policies, curriculum, teaching approaches, and modalities. The learning environment you provide must build the capacity and desire in your students to continually learn and develop. This requires you to embrace and to role model learning with passion. To ensure this context of supportive learning, you must engage in continuous quality improvement through assessing and evaluating your curriculum, your assessment approaches, your teaching, and most importantly, yourself.

Teaching and Learning Excellence

To support innovation in teaching and learning excellence at Centennial College, you are challenged to immerse yourself within a learning-centred environment where learning is placed at the centre of

Introduction

everything you do. Centennial's Teaching Excellence (and Learning Innovation) Framework is based on an integration of constructivist (Wu, 2003; McAlpine, 2000), critical (Freire, [1970]2006; hooks, 1994), and adult learning (andragogy) theories (Knowles, 1984), complemented by emerging theoretical perspectives (Blaschke, 2012; Hase and Kenyon, 2000; Corneli and Danoff, 2011). Taken together, these theoretical underpinnings provide a rich foundation for Centennial's Teaching Excellence Framework (Figure 1). This framework is aligned with Centennial's Academic Plan in values, principles, and directions which affirm and enable Centennial as a leader in transformative learning, global citizenship, quality, and accountability, fostering an innovative approach to learner success and teaching excellence. Centennial's Teaching Excellence Framework (Figure 1) has been included below and illustrates the relationship among the nine principal themes contained in the Academic Plan, placing *Leadership and Learning for All* at the centre.

Figure 1: Centennial College Teaching Excellence (and Learning Innovation) Framework

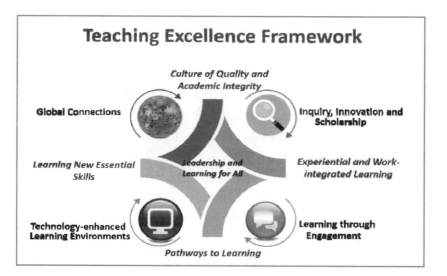

Adapted from:
Centennial College (2013). *Leading through Learning: Academic Plan 2013-2020.*
https://www.centennialcollege.ca/pdf/publications/Academic-Plan.pdf
Pozarnik, B.M. & Lavric, A. (2015). Fostering the quality of teaching and learning by developing the 'neglected half' of university teachers' competencies. *CEPS Journal, 5*(2), 73-93.
Tigelaar, D.E., Dolmans, D.H., Wolfhagen, I.H., & Van Der Vleuten, C.P. (2004). The development and validation of a framework for teaching competencies in higher education. *Higher Education, 48*(2), 253-268.

As a faculty member, you have a responsibility to actively engage with these areas of institutional priority (i.e., Pathways to Learning; Inquiry, Innovation, and Scholarship; Learning New Essential Skills;

Experiential and Work-Integrated Learning; Technology-Enhanced Learning Environments; Global Connections; Learning Through Engagement; Leadership and Learning for All; Culture of Quality and Academic Integrity) as you work towards supporting innovation in teaching and learning excellence. To take action, you must first take a step back and look at the many diverse components of your own teaching practice. Although one of your primary roles is to teach, you may also be providing classroom management, developing assessments, evaluating students, providing advice and guidance, developing curriculum, and supporting quality improvement. With all the roles you play as a faculty member in this dynamic and transformative context, how do you know if you're performing them well?

The College's Strategic Directions – Does Your Work Align?
Centennial College's Strategic Plan underpins and informs all College activities. As a faculty member, it's critical for you to not only have a comprehensive understanding of the College's Strategic Plan, but actively ensure the facilitation of the specific directions and goals through your teaching practice.

Consider the following questions for reflection to check your understanding of the College's Strategic Plan and ways you may contribute to fostering its implementation with your own work.

1. As an academic leader supporting teaching excellence and driving quality forward, what is your level of awareness of the College's Strategic Plan?

   _____
   _____
   _____

2. Think about your current teaching practice. In what ways does it align with the goals outlined in the College's Strategic Plan?

   _____
   _____
   _____

3. Think about where you want to take your teaching practice. What are some concrete strategies you would like to implement to further advance and/or operationalize the goals outlined in the College's Strategic Plan?

   _____
   _____
   _____

The Scholarship of Teaching and Learning

To be a learned scholar of the art of teaching requires thoughtful, intentional, and ongoing analysis of the teaching and learning process. You must recognize that the scholarship of teaching and learning is central to the delivery of high quality curriculum and student engagement in applied, collaborative learning. At Centennial, the Framework for the Scholarship of Teaching and Learning (SoTL) provides context for this work (Figure 2).

Figure 2: Centennial College Framework for the Scholarship of Teaching and Learning (SoTL)

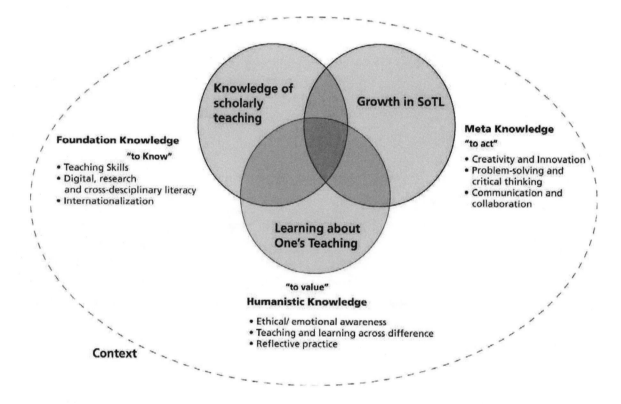

Adapted from:
Randall, N., Heaslip, P., & Morrison, D. (2013). *Campus-based educational development & professional learning: Dimensions & directions.* Vancouver, BC: BCcampus;
Kereluik, K., Mishra, P., Fahnoe, C., & Terry, L. (2013). What knowledge is of most worth: Teacher knowledge for 21st century learning. *Journal of Digital Learning in Teacher Education, 29*(4), 127-140.

The SoTL includes three overlapping and dynamic elements of teaching/learning practice: (1) knowledge of scholarly teaching; (2) learning about one's teaching; and (3) growth in SoTL. The three domains are represented in a Venn diagram illustrating points of intersection and overlap. The framework incorporates:

- *Foundation knowledge* – what faculty "know" – demonstrated through teaching skills, research, cross-disciplinary literacy, and capacity to internationalize and Indigenize curriculum.
- *Humanistic knowledge* – what faculty "value" – inherent characteristics that impact teaching and learning such as ethical and emotional awareness, cultural humility, and ongoing reflexivity.
- *Meta-knowledge* – how faculty "act" – skills and abilities such as creativity and innovation, problem solving and critical reflection, and communication and collaboration across disciplines.

To understand what we mean by 'scholarship' within this framework, it is helpful to look to Boyer's Model of Teaching and Scholarship and its broader definition of scholarship. According to Boyer, there are four types of scholarship:

- *Discovery:* traditional view of scholarship, primary research, quantitative and qualitative data collection, analysis and dissemination.
- *Integration:* interdisciplinary collaboration, critical analysis, review of knowledge, synthesis of views.
- *Application:* knowledge and skills applied to the solution of societal needs and practice gaps.
- *Teaching:* sharing knowledge, reflective analysis of teaching and learning, the product of the scholarships of discovery, integration, and application.

Boyer recognizes these types of scholarship as equal forms of scholarly inquiry (Healey, 2000, Richlin, 2001). By acknowledging these forms of scholarship as equal counterparts, Boyer has transformed the ways in which faculty understand scholarship and research, and engage together as a community of learners and scholars. In relation to the SoTL, Boyer argued that good teaching in itself needs to be better understood, open to critique, and shared with others (Boyer, 1991 in Healey, 2001).

While teaching is defined as *"making student learning possible"*, scholarly teaching is defined as *"making transparent how we have made learning possible"* (Ramsden, 1992, in Healey, 2001). Faculty who engage in scholarly teaching do so explicitly through the three domains of the SoTL framework: (1) knowledge of scholarly teaching ("engaging with the scholarly contributions of others on teaching and learning"); (2) awareness and reflection on one's own teaching practice; and (3) growth in SoTL ("communication and dissemination of aspects of practice and theoretical ideas about teaching and learning in general, and teaching and learning within the discipline") (Healey, 2001:171). In short, a scholarship for teaching is fostered when faculty are able to share their work publicly, receive critique or peer review, and engage in knowledge exchange with their peers and other professional communities (Shulman, 2000 in Luddeke, 2003).

So where do you go next? How can you as a faculty member begin to engage in scholarly teaching? How can you inform, evaluate, and plan your personal journey through the SoTL while exploring and contributing to scholarship as envisioned by Boyer? Consider the power and utility of reflective practice!

Becoming a Reflective Practitioner

Reflective practice is defined as *"the capacity to reflect on action so as to engage in a process of continuous learning"* (Schön, 1983). Reflective practice assumes that individuals, as professionals and teachers, have a high level of commitment, ability, and insight to reflect on what they do, how they do it, and how they might change (Larrivee, 2000). The focus is on self-direction and self-evaluation to seek improvement and increase effectiveness. Reflective practice is a tool that can provide you with the information necessary to guide action towards personal growth and development.

Reflective practice has become a guiding philosophy across several helping professions including science, nursing, medicine, law, and of course, teaching (Loughran, 2002). Helping practitioners are encouraged to question and investigate all aspects of their role to develop an enhanced understanding of their profession, sustain competence, and exercise good judgement in their day-to-day practice (Day, 1999; Smyth, 1992). In the field of teaching, reflective practice has become the gold standard following work by Schön (1983, 1987, 1992), who first linked the concept of reflection to teaching practice. Following Schön, the literature has proliferated, reaffirming the centrality of reflection to good teaching practice (Brookfield, 1995, 2005; Valli, 1992, Zeichner & Liston, 1996).

So why is reflective practice in teaching so important? As a faculty member, you are responsible for preparing a diverse student body for a demanding and dynamic workplace environment. To help students stay current (or ahead of the curve), you need to critically examine your values and biases, how your teaching can support change, how you can provide a quality learning experience, and ways you can show respect for difference (Zeichner & Liston, 1996). Reflective practice can help keep your biases in check, problem-solve, and question the structures that may support or hold back students (Jay & Johnson, 2002). Reflective practice among educators has also been shown to have a direct impact on preparing students for the 'real world'. Mann and colleagues (2007) found that learning environments can have an inhibiting or encouraging effect on supporting reflection and reflective thinking among learners. An important factor to creating a supportive environment was the behaviour of the mentor or supervisor and their ability to model self-reflection. If your primary role as a faculty is to prepare students for a workplace environment that will likely demand them to be reflective practitioners themselves, as an educator, you need to role model these skills within and beyond the classroom environment.

How to Engage in Reflective Practice

By its very nature, self-reflection is an individual activity. However, self-reflection can be further enhanced by the powerful feedback sourced from others including your students, faculty peers, fellow professionals or practitioners in your discipline or subject area, and academic management leaders. This is called 'formative evaluation' since it is aimed at ongoing, process-oriented learning and development.

There are many ways you can collect feedback regarding your effectiveness as a teacher. Tools can include standardized course evaluations such as a *Class Climate* tool which Centennial College initiated at the institutional-level for all courses. Course evaluations are useful as they can provide broad and generalized feedback on your course(s) success and support the institution in collecting metrics on student satisfaction. However, course evaluations can be limiting in providing you with the detail and direction necessary to make substantial changes to your teaching practice. While it is reassuring to receive satisfactory scores from course evaluations, it may be difficult to continually improve teaching practice with little insight as to how improvements can be implemented. Another common source of feedback regarding your teaching practice are statistics on course retention. Unfortunately, you receive this data post-course leaving you no time to make changes that could have impacted a specific cohort of learners. This data also does not answer the critical question – why are students failing your course?

Developing your full potential as a faculty member requires deep and personal reflection and an openness to fully listen (including with your heart), critically process, and implement others' feedback with humility and appreciation. This manual provides you with a compilation of tools and ideas to assist you with this process. The goal of these tools is to provide you with data for your own reflective practice to help you understand how your teaching is perceived by others (e.g., students and colleagues), give you insight into your teaching, and allow you to pause and reflect on questions you may not have previously considered.

Having an improved understanding of your strengths and challenges will help you become more personally aware and effective in all your roles as a faculty member. By using this manual for your own reflections, and the tools within it to gather insights from others, you will be able to develop a practical and powerful action plan to guide you on your journey to mastering the art of teaching.

How to Use the Manual

There is no right or wrong way to use the tools in this manual. Our intention is to offer you a wide range of resources for your own individual reflective practice. By seeking structured feedback from those around you, you will be able to broaden your understanding of how your intentions and actions are perceived by others. By reflecting on your strengths and your areas for continued development, you will start to construct a personalized 'roadmap' for growth. This is an ongoing and never-ending journey: no matter how many months, years or decades of experience that you bring to your faculty role, there is always more to learn!

You may be interested in gathering data from your students, your colleagues or your Chairperson. Alternatively, you may want to focus on a single aspect of your role. Remember, the choice is yours. Revisit this selection of tools throughout your career and try something new. In time, you will find that it is valuable to re-use tools that you have tried out in the past as students change and as you grow and develop. Aldous Huxley once noted that, "*Each ceiling, when reached, becomes a floor.*" In other words, no matter how much we know and do, there is always a new level to which we can aspire to reach.

This manual will provide you with an opportunity to see how each of the tools and activities fit within the domains of Centennial's Framework for the Scholarship of Teaching and Learning (SoTL). This will help you in planning for your scholarly activities and enhance your understanding of the theory that underpins the work you are engaged with. As a reminder, we have provided the following icons beside each of the tools and activities so you can see where they are situated within the framework.

	Knowledge of Scholarly Teaching (Foundation Knowledge): foundational knowledge in teaching skills, demonstration of digital, research and cross-disciplinary literacy and have an awareness of the global context in which your teaching is situated.
	Learning about One's Teaching (Humanistic Knowledge): demonstrate a strong values-based approach to teaching practice including ethical/emotional awareness, teaching and learning across difference, and reflective practice.
	Growth in SoTL (Meta-Knowledge): personal growth in SoTL as it relates to creativity and innovation, problem-solving and critical thinking, and communication and collaboration.

Throughout this manual, we will share personal stories and key learnings from faculty. We hope that these reflections provide you with a snapshot of some of the ways we have implemented the suggested activities and tools into our own teaching practice. In addition, to personal reflections from faculty, we have also given you the opportunity to further reflect on completing an activity or using a suggested tool under the *Your Reflections* sections. We have also included a question in each of these sections which will help you link your findings to the domains of the SoTL framework. If you use a tool or revisit an activity, consider answering these reflective questions again so you can compare your responses and build upon past learning.

As you embark on becoming a reflective practitioner, consider the following quote by Alan Cohen, *"Everyone and everything that shows up in our life is a reflection of something that is happening inside of us."* You have the power within yourself to guide your reflective practice journey. This manual is your map, but only you can be the compass. Time to take the first step!

Figure 3: My Reflective Practice Journey

Part One: Getting Started

"They don't remember what you teach them. They remember what you are."

- Jim Henson

In this section, you will learn more about teaching excellence and the ways that your own values can inform your teaching practice. You will have an opportunity to practice the following activities:
- Reflections on Teaching Excellence
- Identifying Your Ideal Teaching Self

This section will end with an opportunity for reflection and planning to implement your values into your teaching practice.

What Does Teaching Excellence Mean to You?

Ultimately the goal of any reflective practice is to identify what you are doing well and where you would like to make improvements. For this to be an effective and useful process, it is necessary to have a goal in mind. Consider the following questions for personal reflection:

1. What does an excellent teacher look like?

_____

_____

_____

2. What are the characteristics, attributes and skills that make them excellent?

_____

_____

_____

3. What does this teacher do in their practice that other, less effective teachers do not do?

_____

_____

_____

Sue Wells, Lisa McCaie, Megan Barker & Marilyn Herie

Although definitions for teaching excellence vary in the literature, Centennial has developed a framework of teaching excellence competencies which you can use to think about your own teaching practice. The Teaching Excellence and Quality Framework (TEQF) is based on quality assurance standards (Grabove et al., 2012) and research literature focused on 21st Century teaching competencies and quality dimensions in higher education (Johnson et al., 2016; Pozarnik & Lavric, 2015; Fullan and Langworthy, 2013; Van Der Worf and Sabatier, 2009; Tigelaar, et al., 2004). Nine foundational teaching competencies were identified from the research literature (i.e., Learning Facilitator; Curriculum and Assessment Contributor; Content Expert; Lifelong Learner and Scholar; Communicator and Collaborator; Entrepreneur; Knowledge Curator; Global and Digital Citizen; Academic Leader), and have been mapped for your reference below (Figure 4):

Figure 4: Centennial College Teaching Excellence Competencies

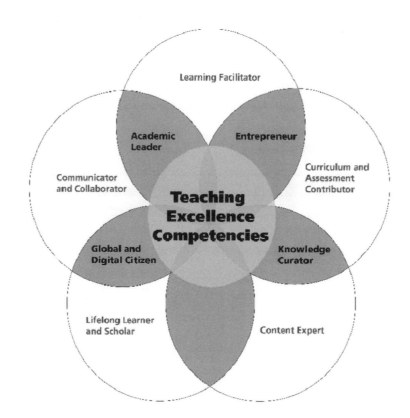

Tigelaar, 2004: 256
Pozannik & Lawnic, 2015: 78-79

In the next few activities, you will begin to think about your personal definition of teaching excellence. As you go through the activities, refer back to the Teaching Excellence and Quality Framework for additional inspiration. Does your definition of teaching excellence include any of the above foundational teaching competencies? What may be new or different with your own definition?

Activity 1: Reflections on Teaching Excellence

In this first activity, you will be asked to reflect on your understanding of teaching excellence. This activity will require you to think back to your own experience as a learner and how it has shaped your own career as a teacher. Try responding to the questions provided below. Remember, the more detailed and rich your responses are, the more you will learn from the activity!

1. Pause for a moment and consider a time in your life when you experienced a 'great' teacher. What was it about this teacher that made them so memorable?

_____

_____

_____

Lisa's thoughts...
Although I am now a faculty, I also attended Centennial as a student and as such I remember my first time walking into Cindy Brandon's classroom (Early Childhood Educator faculty). She warmly greeted each student as we walked in. Each class was filled with knowledge, interesting activities and wonderful conversations. Cindy had high standards and truly believed that her students could meet these standards. However, what set Cindy apart was her passion, excitement and enthusiasm. Throughout the semester, I often found myself observing and 'studying' how Cindy taught. I also realized that I worked extra hard in her class because I admired her. I remember her asking me to keep a sample of my assignment to place in her "excellence" files. I was thrilled!

2. Conversely, consider a time in your life when you experienced a 'poor' teacher. What was it about this teacher or their approach that didn't work for you?

_____

_____

_____

Lisa's thoughts...
This teacher was disorganized and difficult to learn from. The class content was presented poorly, using a lot of lecturing methods in a monotone voice and reading from the textbook. Questions were not welcomed or encouraged. Students were bored in this classroom and the attendance was poor. The assignments expectations were vague and unclear. The feedback

on assignments were minimal at best and no suggestions for improvement were provided. Plus, assignments were not graded and returned in a timely manner. The teacher made no attempt to connect with the students. Unfortunately, I found myself observing what not to do and reflecting on the impact poor teaching has on student success.

3. Reflecting on your answers to these questions, how do you think these experiences have influenced your own teaching?

_____

_____

_____

Lisa's thoughts…
Both experiences have had a significant impact on my current teaching practice. I have come to realize that the teacher is the most important component to the learning process for students. A 'good' teacher can make class content (even 'dry' content) come alive, while a 'poor' teacher can make interesting class content become boring and dull. I have also learned that when teachers make the effort to connect with their students, students will do better! It makes me think of Theodore Roosevelt's quote, *"Nobody cares how much you know, until they know how much you care."*

4. What are three words you would use to describe an excellent teacher?
   i.   _____
   ii. _____
   iii. _____

Lisa's thoughts…
   i.   Caring
   ii. Passionate
   iii. Committed

What Values Do You Bring to Your Role as Faculty?

Fundamental to being a reflective practitioner is identifying the values that you bring to your teaching practice. This is an essential beginning, as it provides a strong foundation for all of your actions and can offer a reference point to guide your reflective practice journey.

Q

Activity 2: Your Ideal Teaching Self

What are the top five values that are most important to you? At this point you may find it easier to reflect on the values that inform your teaching practice. In *Part Three* of this manual, you will have an opportunity to consider if these same values inform how you engage with the other roles you may play as a faculty member when you're outside of the classroom.

In the checklist below, select the words that resonate most with you as a teacher, and/or add others that fit with your goals. What words would you like students to use to describe your teaching? Check off as many as you like. Afterwards, take a second look at the items you identified and circle the top five values that are the most important to you in your day-to-day teaching. Although these words are important to your reflective practice, don't spend too long trying to pick them. Trust your first instinct!

What are the top five values that are the most important to your teaching?

☐ Quality	☐ Respect	☐ Autonomy
☐ Honesty	☐ Service	☐ Integrity
☐ Achievement	☐ Stewardship	☐ Involvement
☐ Empowerment	☐ Wisdom	☐ Objectivity
☐ Balance	☐ Inclusion	☐ Openness
☐ Competence	☐ Authenticity	☐ Influence
☐ Commitment	☐ Reliability	☐ Accountability
☐ Courage	☐ Teamwork	☐ Passionate
☐ Cooperation	☐ Advocacy	☐ Learning-centered
☐ Creativity	☐ Curiosity	☐ Transformative
☐ Discipline	☐ Acceptance	☐ Equitable
☐ Flexibility	☐ Balance	☐ Ethical
☐ Integrity	☐ Inspirational	☐ Agile
☐ Perseverance	☐ Compassion	☐ Collaborative
☐ Order	☐ Innovation	☐ Accessible
☐ Other _____	☐ Other _____	☐ Other _____
☐ Other _____	☐ Other _____	☐ Other _____

> **Lisa's thoughts...**
> My core values are: commitment, respect, inclusion, inspirational and passionate, learning-centered.

Now that you have identified the core values that inform your teaching, write a definition for each of the words that you selected. Think more about what these values mean to you.

Using the lines below, write down your top core values and provide a short definition for each value:

1. _____
_____
_____

2. _____
_____
_____

3. _____
_____
_____

4. _____
_____
_____

5. _____
_____
_____

> **Lisa's thoughts...**
> *Commitment*: investing time and energy on an ongoing basis to work towards becoming the best teacher possible for students, for my colleagues, the field of Early Childhood Education, and for Centennial.
>
> *Respect*: treating people the way you would like them to treat you in a professional and personal manner.

Inclusion: creating opportunities to include everyone in an authentic manner. To create environments where everyone has a sense of belonging, accessibility, and respect.

Inspirational and Passionate: strong feelings and emotions are expressed and used as motivation to excel.

Learner-centered: to meet the students where they are at in the learning process and to support their journey of learning to a higher level in a collaborative manner.

Think about your experience defining your values using the following questions as a guide:

1. How difficult or easy was it for you to define your foundational values? Explain.

    _____

    _____

    _____

2. Where do your values come from? This could include examples you have seen modeled, cultural values, your upbringing, teaching experience, media representation, faith beliefs, professional development, etc.

    _____

    _____

    _____

3. What did this process reveal to you about the teacher that you aspire to be?

    _____

    _____

    _____

Lisa's thoughts….
This process revealed that my values often match my teaching practice which makes me feel proud of my work!

Operating from your Values

So far, you have identified the values that underpin your work, the kind of faculty member you currently are and aspire to be, and created your own personal definitions for the values that are important to you. You will want to refer to your work in this section throughout the rest of this manual, as you continuously link your values to your ongoing reflective practice and learning.

Our values inform how we see ourselves. Our collective challenge is to act in ways that express these values every day so that they shine through to those around us. If we can succeed at this, we model a powerful ethic of integrity that has the power to be instilled in our students, our colleagues, even the leaders we look up to.

Your Reflections

Take a moment to reflect on completing the activities in *Part One* of this manual and how they will impact your teaching practice. Questions for reflection follow Lisa's example below.

Lisa's thoughts...
I will demonstrate my values today by:
- Starting the day with inspiration (e.g., find a quote, watch a short inspirational video, engage in a small random act of kindness every day for at least one person, etc.).

- Making connections with students inside and outside the classroom (e.g., share observations, ask questions, provide affirmations, etc.).

- Reflecting on what is working or not working. Giving myself a grade after every class.

- Using informal and formal student feedback to guide my practice (e.g., one minute papers, check-ins, conversations/discussions, and personal observations of students in the classroom).

- Acknowledging accomplishments at the end of the day and celebrating them!

1. How will you demonstrate your values today?

_____

_____

_____

2. What is your personal signature as a teacher?

_____

_____

_____

3. How can you more explicitly link your values to your personal signature as a teacher?

_____

_____

_____

4. SoTL: How will this impact what you know, what you value, and how you will act (i.e., impact on your scholarly teaching and/or contributions to teaching and learning scholarship)?

_____

_____

_____

Lisa's thoughts…

I believe that the most effective teachers can bring something unique to their class, style, or to the techniques used. These teachers can connect with students and inspire them by going above and beyond the expectations of their role. They can spark interest and eagerness in their students to want more. Students remember these unique experiences for many years and often relate them to a love of learning. Highly effective teachers will over time create an identity for themselves based on the uniqueness and creativity of their style.

Years ago, I read a short story from Chicken Soup for the Soul (Canfield & Victor Hansen, 1996) that changed the way I teach today. This story was about a man with special needs who worked in a grocery store bagging groceries. The manager of the store noticed that customers were waiting in a long line to pay for their groceries. He offered them another cashier to speed up the process. To his surprise, the customers did not want to make the change because they wanted to have their groceries bagged by the man with special needs. When asked why, the customers said that the man with special needs always packed his groceries bags beautifully, made special connections with the customers by asking questions and engaging in a conversation, and that he always placed a hand-written note with a special message of gratitude. The manager of the store was shocked that he wrote these notes for years and placed them in each customer's grocery bags. These notes were described as his 'personal signature', a kind gesture that made him unique. This story made me ask myself, *"What is my personal signature?"*

I have always loved quotes as I find a lot of inspiration from them. I knew that I wanted to incorporate my love for quotes to create my own 'personal signature'. I decided that I would start each class with a small treat for the students with an inspirational quote. These have included:

- Hustle and heart...will set you apart! (with a heart-shaped candy)
- Let's wiggle our way into another assignment. (with a gummy worm)
- Having a positive attitude can be a life saver. (with a life saver)
- Your education is priceless. (with a chocolate coin)

I had no idea just how these candy quotes would impact my student's lives. I am told all the time just how much the students appreciate them and how it makes them feel cared for. Many students have shared that they keep the quotes from first semester until their final semester. Some students share it with their children and many of their children know me as the 'candy teacher'. Many students post their candy quotes on social media. I have an international student who mails them to her family. Some students keep them in a special place like posting them on the bathroom mirror to look at every morning, in journals, on the cover of their class binders, in their pencil cases, etc.

My favorite story comes from a colleague who I gave a candy quote to as he interviewed me. During a visit with his mother who is living with Alzheimer's, he gave the candy quote to her. The following day, his mother found the candy quote sitting on her table. She thought that the candy quote was given to her by a secret admirer, as she had forgotten it was her son who gave it to her. He said that this candy quote has given his mother joy and excitement each day she sees it.

Paola's thoughts...
My core values are Reliability, Inspirational, Passionate, Ethical and Collaborative.

The main thing that this process revealed to me is the congruency between my professional and personal values. I have integrated what I have learned and experienced in the field into my work as a professor, to give students an idea of the expectations that are involved in being a Child and Youth Care Practitioner, and continue to grow and develop – meaning the work is never complete!

Part Two: A Deeper Dive – How Are You Teaching?

"The mediocre teacher tells. The good teacher explains. The superior teacher demonstrates. The great teacher inspires."

- William A. Ward

In this section, you will learn more about what your teaching practice truly looks like from different points of view (e.g., yourself, your students, your colleagues, and your Chairperson). You will have an opportunity to practice the following activities:

- Guiding Beliefs Survey
- Cross Check
- Testing and Teaching – Is it a Match?
- Call a Friend
- Did You Meet the Outcomes?
- Let's Make the Next 7 Weeks Even Better
- Benchmark of Online Teaching Excellence
- Is Your Classroom Inclusive?
- Student Focus Group

This section will incorporate multiple opportunities for reflection and planning as you set goals to enhance your own teaching practice.

Data Collection Tools: Focus on Teaching

Feedback on your teaching can be provided through several quantitative as well as qualitative indicators which may include how your academic program scores on college-wide Key Performance Indicators, student course evaluations, and course retention. These tools and metrics are useful as broad indicators of teaching success. However, to collect feedback on the full scope of your teaching practice, you may consider incorporating additional tools which can provide more granular and individualized feedback to support learning and development.

This section contains a variety of tools that you can use to collect data about your effectiveness as a teacher. Your other faculty roles of student advising, designing assessments, program review etc., will be addressed in *Part Three* of this manual. The tools in this section will help you to take 'a deeper dive' and collect information that is directly related to your teaching practice. This data will help you to reflect on what you are doing, how well you are doing it, and how you might improve.

These data collection tools are not meant to be used in sequence or all at one time. Select one or two tools that resonate with you right now and return periodically to this section of the manual to try something new. As you review the tools and exercises, think about how you may use these tools to elicit feedback about your personal style and how it can impact changes in your teaching.

Personalized Guiding Beliefs Survey for Teachers

At the heart of being an effective teacher is your ability to identify the beliefs that guide your practice. The next activity uses the core values you identified as a starting point for you to create a more in-depth data collection tool to assess your teaching effectiveness.

Q

Activity 3: The Guiding Beliefs Survey

This activity invites you to outline the principles that guide your teaching and elicit from others the extent to which your values are reflected in your approach to teaching. To do this, you need to reflect on the core values you outlined in *Part One* of this manual and identify how you would like to operationalize these values in practice. Upon reflection and implementation, you can share these personalized guiding beliefs with students through a customized survey. Remember to be open to receiving both positive and negative feedback. This may feel risky, but this exercise could provide you with some of the most valuable insights you have ever received! You can create your own *Guiding Beliefs Survey* through the steps outlined below.

Step One: Your Core Values in Five Words or Less

Select the core values you identified in *Part One, Activity 2: Your Ideal Teaching Self,* of this manual and record them down the side of the chart provided below. These words will act as powerful anchors as you develop your own survey.

Step Two: Stating the Ideal

Reflecting on each value, create a sentence that describes your ideal way of teaching. Think about how you would like your students to see you and what you would like them to say about your approach to teaching.

This exercise can be challenging. It asks you to 'dig deep' and reflect on what you do, how you do it, and the ways in which others perceive how you do it. Below is an example of how Lisa linked together the key words that represent her core values and her explanations for the guiding beliefs behind each of the values.

Lisa's thoughts...	
Core Value (select one key world)	**How You Would Like Others to See that Value in Action (Your Guiding Belief)**
Commitment	I hope that students see my commitment to their success starting with the first day of classes. Then I hope that students can see specific examples of my commitment throughout the semester.
Respect	I hope that students see my efforts in creating classrooms where respect is modeled, encouraged, practiced and discussed.
Inclusion	I hope that all students feel a sense of belonging within a safe learning environment in my courses. I would like all students to feel that they can approach me for an open discussion to ensure that their individual needs are met in a group setting.
Inspiration	I understand that I have the opportunity to inspire both inside and outside of the classroom. I am often inspired by others including my students and take the time to let them know in a variety of creative ways.
Passionate	I would hope students see my passion every time I interact with them as well as my passion for children and the field of Early Childhood Education.
Learner-centered	During the first class, I explain to students that I want them to be the best Registered Early Childhood Educator (RECE) that they can be because children deserve the best! I inform them that I have high expectations but I believe that if we work together in collaboration that we can achieve these expectations. Throughout the semester, students should be able to see evidence of collaboration.

Now it's your turn! Complete the following table with your own values and guiding beliefs, based on your teaching practice and reflections.

Core Value (select one key world)	How You Would Like Others to See that Value in Action (Your Guiding Belief)

Step Three: Designing Your Survey

For the last step in this activity, you will use your responses from the previous two steps (see above) to develop personalized survey questions. In the text box below, Lisa has provided a sample of her own survey which she then used to collect feedback from her students. Feel free to repurpose the content from Lisa's survey if it aligns with your own beliefs. You can also create your own.

Note: You may prefer to send the survey to students using an online data collection tool (e.g., Survey Monkey), to preserve respondent's anonymity. You may decide to make all or some of the questions qualitative (i.e., open-ended responses) or quantitative (i.e., scaling questions to elicit numeric ratings). Just make sure that the questions allow your students to assess how your values align with your actions as a teacher.

Lisa's thoughts...

Dear Students,
I would love your input! As a part of my reflective practice, I would love some feedback to see if my core values are being effectively implemented in the classroom. Please be honest as I really want to know what is working well and what I could be doing differently. Thank you in advance! - Lisa

Core Value: COMMITMENT
I am committed to helping you to be educated and to succeed in this course
1. What is working well?
2. What could I do differently?
3. How has this core value impacted you as a student or in your life?

Core Value: RESPECT
I respect you as my student and a member of this classroom environment
1. What is working well?
2. What could I do differently?
3. How has this core value impacted you as a student or in your life?

Core Value: INCLUSION
It is important for me that everyone feels that they belong and are welcomed in this class
1. What is working well?
2. What could I do differently?
3. How has this core value impacted you as a student or in your life?

Core Value: INSPIRATION & PASSIONATE
I hope that you can see my passion and feel inspired in every class
1. What is working well?
2. What could I do differently?
3. How has this core value impacted you as a student or in your life?

Core Value: LEARNER-CENTERED
I want us to work together in collaboration
1. What is working well?
2. What could I do differently?
3. How has my core values impacted you as a student or in your life?

Your Reflections

Take a moment to think about your experience putting the survey together and receiving feedback from your students. You can use the following questions as a guide:

1. What did you learn about yourself from this activity? What surprised you?

_____

_____

_____

2. What do you do well? (It is OK to congratulate yourself!)

_____

_____

_____

3. What change(s) would you like to consider right now? In the future?

_____

_____

_____

4. SoTL: How will this impact what you know, what you value, and how you will act (i.e., impact on your scholarly teaching and/or contributions to teaching and learning scholarship)?

_____

_____

_____

Reflecting on Your Teaching Style

In *Part One* of this manual, you identified and described your core values, words that you would like students to use to describe your teaching. The key words that you used to identify your core values should be implemented in your day-to-day teaching and modeled to those around you.

Activity 4: Cross Check

In this activity, you will ask others (i.e., students, your colleagues, and your Chairperson) to describe your teaching style using a few key words. You can introduce the activity to these groups of people by letting them know that you are committed to success in your teaching practice. You can also let them know that their feedback will give you a 'snapshot' of what you are doing well and where there is room for improvement.

Note: To ensure open and honest feedback, you may consider asking for feedback anonymously. For example, leave a box or basket at the front of your classroom or in your office so that students, colleagues or your Chairperson can provide their feedback anonymously. You can also ask someone to collect the feedback on your behalf.

Step One: Your Students

First, find out what your students think. Ask your students what words they would use to describe you and your values as a teacher. Once you collect their feedback, reflect using the following question as a guide:

How does their perspective fit with yours? Is there an area (value) that you feel you could bring forward, make more visible and tangible to others?

_____

_____

_____

Lisa's thoughts….
Our perspectives were a close match, as the traits about my teaching that stood out the most of my students (passion, etc.) were traits that I work really hard to incorporate into my classes. A lot of my students noted that they feel like they have a voice in my classroom, and I think that I could show my value of student input even more by offering more choices in my classroom, such as using different sources of technology that allow students to state their thoughts and opinions.

Paola's thoughts…
For this exercise, I asked students to list three words that they felt described my teaching style or values.

While I am always reflecting and incorporating new techniques to enhance my teaching, I am pleased with the fact that students viewed my teaching style so positively. While they strayed slightly from the values and focused more on the teaching style, I appreciated their feedback and can tie in the words they used to my values and teaching style.

I can be hard on myself, and in doing so I don't always capture the positives. I am thankful that my students can see this, and reviewing some of the descriptions they gave, I have many strengths to reflect on. Students can be very literal, and can sense when someone is not being genuine. Seeing some of the words they used to describe my teaching, I feel I may sell my strengths short, and that I have a greater impact on students than I realize.

Step Two: Your Colleagues
Next, explore your colleague's point of view. At a team meeting, hand out blank slips of paper and ask your team to individually (and anonymously) write down three words that they think describe your teaching style. Once you collect their feedback, reflect using the following question as a guide:

How does their perspective fit with yours? Is there an area (value) that you feel you could bring forward, make more visible, and tangible to others?

_____

_____

_____

Lisa's thoughts….
Our perspectives were slightly different. Most of the values that were used to describe me are values in my life, but not the four most important values that I selected. They said that I am creative, reflective, organized, and thoughtful. I can make my ability to be organized even more visible by sharing some of the strategies that I have found most helpful in staying organized with my co-workers.

Step Three: Your Chairperson

Finally, consider your Chairperson's perspective. At your next meeting with your Chairperson, ask them what words they would use to describe you and your values as a teacher. Once you collect their feedback, reflect using the following question as a guide:

How does their perspective fit with yours? Is there an area (value) that you feel you could bring forward, make more visible, and tangible to others?

_____

_____

_____

Lisa's thoughts….
My Chairperson selected a total of four core values to describe my teaching. Two were slightly different core values (authenticity and accessible) than the ones I selected for myself. However, I was very pleased to know that she thinks of my skills in this way as they are wonderful values to have. Based on this experience, I found myself further evaluating my authenticity and accessible values and challenged myself to think about how I implement these values into practice.

Once you collect feedback from these three groups, compare this feedback to your own core values using the following questions as a guide:

1. How do the values provided by others fit with your own list of core values?

_____

_____

_____

2. Based on the feedback provided, explain how you think your students, colleagues, and Chairperson see you.

_____

_____

_____

3. Reflect on the areas of strength you missed but others noted and the areas they identified that you don't necessarily agree with.

_____

_____

_____

Christine's thoughts…

I chose a portion of the cross check to pilot, just to get my feet wet. In this Cross Check tool, it asks you to have your team jot down three words that describe your teaching style. I decided to ask the entire office because I feel we all support and inspire each other in so many ways and therefore have a direct impact on each other's teaching.

Here is what my 'team' had to say:

Other faculty reflection tools such as *Class Climate* are valuable in some ways. However, I find that while there are a lot of positives written by the students I tend to focus more on anything negative and take it personally. This activity was a real 'ah ha' moment for me because it really solidified my own core values that I try to illustrate in the classroom and amongst my colleagues.

As I started to receive words back from my team I instantly felt motivated and renewed. I think it is important that we are not only supporting our students but our colleagues as well. I am fortunate to have a team who cheers each other on!

Your Reflections

Upon completing this activity, reflect on your experience receiving feedback using the following questions as a guide:

1. What did you learn about yourself from this activity? What surprised you?

_____

_____

_____

2. What do you do well? (It is OK to congratulate yourself!)

_____

_____

_____

3. What change(s) would you like to consider right now? In the future?

_____

_____

_____

4. SoTL: How will this impact what you know, what you value, and how you will act (i.e., impact on your scholarly teaching and/or contributions to teaching and learning scholarship)?

_____

_____

_____

> **Lisa's thoughts...**
> This activity made me proud as I learned that the values that I strive to incorporate into my teaching have come across to my students. For example, my students can tell how committed I am to helping them find success. I also realized that I am better at celebrating others then being celebrated myself as receiving positive feedback is sometimes uncomfortable for me.

Sue Wells, Lisa McCaie, Megan Barker & Marilyn Herie

Student Assessments and Your Teaching Practice

When you assess students in your courses, you would typically align tests, assignments, lab work, simulations, or other activities with the course-level and program-level learning outcomes. This can help you gauge students' mastery of applied knowledge and skills. However, students' performance on your assessments can also be a valuable tool for learning more about your teaching practice and providing insight into how effective you were in facilitating their learning. While there are many factors that can impact a student's academic success (e.g., academic readiness, study skills, health, life responsibilities, learning or other limitations or needs), it's important to remember that *how well you taught* will always play a role.

Activity 5: Testing and Teaching – Is it a Match?
In this activity, you will follow a series of steps to analyze your students' outcomes on an assessment that you have administered. This will provide you with an opportunity to see how these outcomes may be connected to your approach to teaching. This activity could be completed individually or completed in conjunction with faculty colleagues who teach different sections of the same course.

Step One: Choose an Assignment or Test

Review your class success rates on the assessments administered in your course. Try to focus on an assessment with a high fail rate or where the distribution of grades is skewed towards the lower range. With any assessment, there is generally a range of grades achieved by the students. Sometimes it is the distribution of this range that will provide you with valuable information. Remember, there will always be students in your classes who will do well with little support and coaching on your part. The students in your class that have more difficulty will likely respond to different teaching styles or approaches which may not always be aligned with your own style. For the students that struggled with your chosen assessment, pay attention to what they are telling you about your teaching practice through their results. How could you have supported them better? What could you have done differently to ensure a better outcome? You may also want to pay attention to the assessments where students' grades clustered tightly at the higher end of the distribution.

Step Two: Look Closer…and Closer

Within the assessment, identify where students lost the most marks. Is there a concept that they struggled with, a task they couldn't master, directions that could have been clearer, or a common error made by many students? What are the patterns that emerge as you dig deeper into the results?

Step Three: Reflect on Your Teaching

Now that you have identified patterns, return to your teaching plans and identify where and when you taught specific topics or where students practiced discrete skills that you assessed. Consider the following:

Did you teach the concept or was it only in the textbook?

Did your teaching approach cater to a variety of learning styles (i.e., visual, auditory and/or kinesthetic)? Did your approach match the learners in your classroom?

Did you teach the concept at the same level of learning that you expected on the assessment? For example, did you teach at the knowledge level and then test the student's ability to apply it?

How much time did you spend on the topic? Was it comparable to the weighting of the topic in the evaluation?

Could students have benefitted from having more time or activities in your classroom or lab to apply their learning prior to being assessed?

Think back to that day and time. What else was going on in your life that could have contributed to your teaching approach? Were you happy, sad, distracted, stressed etc.? How could the way that you felt have contributed to your student's ability to learn the concepts presented?

Lisa's thoughts….

I have recently rewritten a test for a specific course. I wanted to add more application type questions. I found a short story that fit the class content well and used it for a case study. I wrote five multiple choice questions related to the story and class content. I was surprised how much the students enjoyed this type of testing. Students commented how much they enjoyed reading the short story and were challenged by questions. The results of these questions were that most students who did well overall on the test also did well on these test questions. Students who struggled on these questions, typically also struggled with the test overall.

Your Reflections

Upon completing this activity, reflect on your experience comparing student assessments with your teaching practice using the following questions as a guide:

1. What did you learn about yourself from this activity? What surprised you?

_____

_____

_____

2. What do you do well? (It is OK to congratulate yourself!)

_____

_____

_____

3. What change(s) would you like to consider right now? In the future?

_____

_____

_____

4. SoTL: How will this impact what you know, what you value, and how you will act (i.e., impact on your scholarly teaching and/or contributions to teaching and learning scholarship)?

_____

_____

_____

Navigating the Teaching Journey

Imagine yourself teaching a class. You are in the middle of explaining a key concept and all the while you are thinking about the following:

> *Did I prepare the students for this new concept? Do they understand me? Should I add an example? The student in the back is talking – should I say something? Will I cover everything before the class ends? How is my time?*

Does this feel familiar? That is because teaching is not a linear process. It is more like a road trip – there is a destination in mind but you may get lost, see something you weren't expecting, or add new stops on your journey. In the end, you will arrive at your destination, although navigating the tricky terrain may have been difficult if you were going it alone! In this scenario, wouldn't it be helpful to have a fellow navigator?

Activity 6: Call a Friend

In this activity, you will invite a colleague to observe your class and provide you with feedback. Ideally, this process could be reciprocated with both participants providing feedback to each other. The goal is to receive feedback that can help each of you reflect upon your own teaching practice.

Identifying and asking a colleague to join you in this process is key. Consider the other person's experience, teaching style, and strengths. There is value in selecting someone who you perceive to have a similar style to you. However, do not ignore the potential value of selecting someone who you feel has a different teaching style and may offer unique and thought-provoking insights that can take your teaching practice to the next level.

Prior to approaching a fellow faculty member to join you in this activity consider the various components of your teaching. Which areas would you like your colleague to focus on? Review the following questionnaire and select the areas you would like to explore further.

	TEACHING SKILLS	
A.	**IMPORTANCE AND SUITABILITY OF CONTENT**	
1.	The material covered is generally accepted by industry professionals/practitioners to be relevant	☐
2.	The material is important for this group of students	☐
3.	Students seem to have the necessary background to understand the class material	☐
4.	The examples used drew upon student's experiences	☐
5.	When appropriate, a distinction was made between factual material and opinions	☐
6.	When appropriate, references were cited to support assertions or to source content shared or presented	☐
7.	Sufficient material was included in the class	☐
8.	Content represents current thinking in the discipline	☐
9.	Class material is relevant to course objectives and assigned readings, lab work, co-op or placement experience, etc.	☐
B.	**ORGANIZATION OF CONTENT**	
	Introductory Portion	
1.	Stated purpose of the class	☐
2.	Presented brief overview of the class content	☐
3.	Stated a problem to be solved or discussed during the class	☐
4.	Made explicit the relationship between today's and the previous class	☐
	Body of Class	
1.	Arranged and discussed the content in a systematic and organized fashion that was made explicit to the students	☐
2.	Asked questions periodically to determine whether too much or too little information was being presented	☐
3.	Presented information at an appropriate level of abstraction	☐
4.	Presented examples to clarify very abstract/difficult ideas	☐
5.	Explicitly stated relationship among various ideas	☐
6.	Periodically summarized the most important ideas in the class	☐
7.	Provided a balance of at least 50% of classroom or lab time Spent in experiential learning (application and practice of knowledge and skills), relative to lecturing/presenting	☐
	Conclusion of Class	
1.	Summarized the main ideas	☐

TEACHING SKILLS

2.	Solved or otherwise dealt with any problems that arose during the class	☐
3.	Related the day's class to upcoming classes/events	☐
4.	Restated what students were expected to gain from the class material and how this will inform professional practice	☐

Voice Characteristics

1.	Rate of speech was neither too fast nor too slow	☐
2.	Voice was raised or lowered for variety and emphasis	☐
3.	Speech was neither too formal nor too casual	☐
4.	Speech fillers, for example "okay?", "right", and "umm" were not distracting	☐
5.	Rate of speech was neither too fast nor too slow	☐

Nonverbal Communication

1.	Wasn't too casual in style	☐
2.	Facial and body movements did not contradict speech or expressed intentions. For example, waited for responses after asking questions	☐
3.	Used gestures effectively	☐

General Style

1.	Demonstrated enthusiasm for subject matter	☐
2.	Demonstrated command of subject matter	☐
3.	Modeled professional and ethical behaviour	☐
4.	Used instructional aids to communicate important points	☐

C.   **CLARITY OF PRESENTATION**

1.	Stated purpose at the beginning of the class	☐
2.	Defined new terms, concepts, and principles	☐
3.	Told the students why certain processes, techniques, or formulae were used to solve problems	☐
4.	Used relevant examples to explain major ideas	☐
5.	Used clear and simple examples	☐
6.	Explicitly related new ideas to already familiar ones	☐
7.	Reiterated definitions of new terms to help students become accustomed to them	☐

	TEACHING SKILLS	
8.	Provided occasional summaries and restatements of important ideas	☐
9.	Used alternate explanations when necessary	☐
10.	Slowed the word flow when ideas were complex and difficult	☐
11.	Did not often digress from the main topic	☐
12.	Spoke directly to the class	☐
13.	If used, slides were professional, well-designed, impactful, engaging, referenced appropriately, and complemented spoken content	☐
D.	**ASKING QUESTIONS**	
1.	About the class topic: asked questions to see what the students knew	☐
2.	Addressed questions to individual students as well as group at large	☐
3.	Paused after all questions to allow students time to think	☐
4.	Encouraged students to answer difficult questions by providing cues or rephrasing	☐
5.	When necessary, asked students to clarify their questions	☐
6.	Asked probing questions if a student's answer was incomplete or superficial	☐
7.	Repeated answers when necessary so the entire class could hear	☐
8.	Received student's questions politely and, when possible, enthusiastically	☐
9.	Refrained from answering questions when unsure of a correct response; offered to find the answer with students, or challenged students to find the answer	☐
10.	Requested that very difficult, time-consuming questions of limited interest be discussed before or after class or during office hours	☐
11.	Asked a variety of types of questions (rhetorical, open and closed)	☐
12.	Addressed questions to volunteer and non-volunteer students	☐
E.	**ESTABLISHING AND MAINTAINING CONTACT WITH STUDENTS**	
	Establishing Contact	☐

TEACHING SKILLS

1.	Greeted students with small talk	☐
2.	Established eye contact with as many students as possible	☐
3.	Set ground rules for student participation and questioning	☐
4.	Used questions to gain student attention	☐
5.	Encouraged student's questions and contributions	☐

Maintaining Contact

1.	Maintained eye contact with as many students as possible	☐
2.	Used rhetorical questions to re-engage student attention	☐
3.	Asked questions which allowed the professor to gauge student progress	☐
4.	Answered student's questions satisfactorily	☐
5.	Noted and responded to signs of puzzlement, boredom, curiosity, and so on	☐
6.	Varied the pace of the class to keep students alert	☐
7.	Spoke at a rate which allowed students time to take notes	☐

Now that you have reviewed the checklist above, complete the following table below, outlining the actions you will take:

My Action Plan			
I Would Like to Be Observed and Receive Feedback On:	**The Colleague I Will Ask Is:**	**Date/Time:**	**Outcomes and Lessons Learned:**

A Note about Lecturing...

Is lecturing relevant in today's teaching and learning environments, where students have access to a complete library of all knowledge in their back pocket (i.e., through their mobile device)? Despite advances and adoption of adult learning and student-centered modes of teaching, many faculty members still default to a "chalk and talk", transmission model of teaching.

As part of your reflective practice, challenge yourself to identify alternatives to lecturing, in order to better support students' knowledge construction, peer-to-peer learning, and experiential and applied learning modes.

Here are "57 Alternatives to Lecturing[1]" for your consideration:

Learning Models
1. Self-directed learning
2. Learning through play
3. Scenario-based learning
4. Game-based learning
5. Project-based learning
6. Peer-to-peer instruction
7. School-to-school instruction (e.g., through Skype)
8. Learning through projects
9. Problem-based learning
10. Challenge-based learning
11. Inquiry-based learning
12. Mobile learning
13. Gamified learning (i.e., gamification)
14. Cross-curricular projects
15. Reciprocal Teaching
16. "Flipped-class" learning
17. Face-to-face driver blended learning
18. Rotation blended learning
19. Flex blended learning
20. "Online Lab" blended learning
21. Sync teaching
23. HyFlex learning

---

[1] Included with permission from TeachThought and retrieved from: http://www.teachthought.com/pedagogy/50-alternatives-to-lecturing/

24. Self-guided MOOC
25. Traditional MOOC
26. Competency-based learning
27. Question-based learning

Literacy Strategies
28. Write-around
29. Four corners
30. Accountable talk
31. RAFT assignments
32. Fishbowl
33. Debate
34. Gallery walk
35. Text reduction
36. Concentric circles
37. Traditional concept-mapping (e.g., teacher-given strategy–"fishbone" cause-effect analysis)
38. Didactic, personalized concept-mapping (i.e., student designed and personalized for their knowledge-level and thinking patterns)
39. Mock trial
40. Non-academic video + "academic" questioning
41. Paideia seminar
42. Symposium
43. Socratic seminar
44. QFT strategy
45. Concept attainment
46. Directed reading thinking activity
47. Paragraph shrinking
48. FRAME routine
49. Jigsaw strategy
50. Content-based team-building activities

Your Reflections

Upon completing this activity, reflect on your experience creating an action plan and receiving feedback from a colleague using the following questions as a guide:

1. What did you learn about yourself from this activity? What surprised you?

_____
_____
_____

2. What do you do well? (It is OK to congratulate yourself!)

_____
_____
_____

3. What change(s) would you like to consider right now? In the future?

_____
_____
_____

4. SoTL: How will this impact what you know, what you value, and how you will act (i.e., impact on your scholarly teaching and/or contributions to teaching and learning scholarship)?

_____
_____
_____

Teaching Effectiveness and Learning Outcomes

When you plan a class, you know the route you will take, but can the students follow your map? How do you know if the students reached the destination? As a faculty member, you plan your classes with clear outcomes in mind. You think about what the students will know, understand or be able to demonstrate after the class, and plan the learning activities around specific goals. Your ability to articulate the learning outcomes for a class can provide you with an opportunity to gather 'in-the-moment' feedback on your teaching effectiveness. It can be as simple as letting your students know where you were going and then asking them if they got there too.

Activity 7: Did You Meet the Outcomes?

Many faculty share an agenda with their students at the beginning of the class to let them know what topics will be discussed. However, the agenda does not always outline for students the expected class outcomes. In this activity, you will adjust your class agenda to include learning outcomes. Consider structuring your agenda using the following format:

Today's Agenda
At the end of this class you (the students) will be able to: 1. _____   2. _____   3. _____

Finding out how effective your teaching was that day can be as simple as checking in with your students at the end of the class to see if they think the learning outcomes were met. Consider using the following format:

I am committed to being an effective teacher and helping you to meet the intended learning outcomes. I value your feedback for my reflection and continued improvement. How confident are you that you have achieved today's learning outcomes? Please let me know by rating on a scale where 1 = not confident and 5 = very confident. Please be candid in your responses – this survey is anonymous.

Sue Wells, Lisa McCaie, Megan Barker & Marilyn Herie

After attending this class, how confident are you that you can:

Insert your class outcome

1	2	3	4	5
Not Confident		Neutral		Very confident

Insert your class outcome

1	2	3	4	5
Not Confident		Neutral		Very confident

Insert your class outcome

1	2	3	4	5
Not Confident		Neutral		Very confident

Once completed, review the results from the students and focus on the areas where they reported a low confidence level. You may consider investigating further to determine why students did not feel confident with certain concepts. You may also decide to make changes to how you teach your next class. This activity provides you with valuable information in a timely way, allowing you to make necessary adjustments to your teaching before you progress to more complex topics or introduce new concepts which will build upon these outcomes.

You could also adjust the survey to 'dig 'deeper' into the students' understanding of the learning outcomes by adding open ended questions asking the students to identify the specific classroom experiences that helped them to meet the outcomes. This more detailed information will help you to identify the teaching and learning experiences that your students find most effective.

Lisa's thoughts…
One of the classes that I teach is one that the students tend to find difficult and consequently it has a high failure rate. I am always looking for ways to support their learning in this course and increase the number of students who are successful. With this in mind, I created a study guide that outlined the outcomes for each class. At the beginning of each class, I reviewed the learning outcomes from the study guide. At the end of class, students would be able to make connections between the learning outcomes and the class content. The students were

---

encouraged to highlight their answers in their notes using the learning outcomes. This became their study notes and guide when preparing for exams. This strategy had the following benefits:

- Students have reported feeling more confident and less stressed when writing exams.
- The guide ensures that I am teaching to the learning outcomes on a weekly basis.
- The class average has increased by approximately 10 percent. (i.e. from a C to B grade)
- More students are now passing the course which has improved student retention.

Students are now having more success transferring their learning to second semester. This improvement was reported to me by both the students and my colleagues.

Your Reflections

Upon completing this activity, reflect on your experience outlining learning outcomes with students using the following questions as a guide:

1. What did you learn about yourself from this activity? What surprised you?

_____

_____

_____

2. What do you do well? (It is OK to congratulate yourself!)

_____

_____

_____

3. What change(s) would you like to consider right now? In the future?

_____

_____

_____

4. SoTL: How will this impact what you know, what you value, and how you will act (i.e., impact on your scholarly teaching and/or contributions to teaching and learning scholarship)?

_____

_____

_____

Reflecting Midterm: Successes and Opportunities

Being open to student feedback is an important part of the reflective practice process as it can be very insightful. Student feedback can help us see what is working in our classrooms and explore possibilities of what we could do differently. The mid-way point of the course is an excellent time to pause, take a breath, and reflect.

Activity 8: Let's Make the Next 7 Weeks Even Better

In this activity, you will use the mid-way point of your course to ask students for feedback on what is working for them and what would help to facilitate their learning. This can be done informally through a classroom discussion, however offering the students a confidential way to respond may result in data that is truly reflective of their opinions.

Consider the following list of questions and select one or two that resonate with you to ask the students:

1. Share one suggestion that I could implement (as your teacher) in the next seven weeks to make these classes even better.
2. Share one suggestion that you could implement (as a student or classmate) in the next seven weeks to make these classes even better.
3. Which points in this class have you been most engaged as a learner?
4. Which points in this class have you been least engaged as a learner?
5. What is one thing you would like me to stop doing as your teacher?
6. What is one thing you would like me to start doing as your teacher?
7. What is one thing that is working well that I should continue to do?

The most important part of this activity is your response to the feedback that your students provide. It is crucial that you honestly consider their idea and opinions and let the students know how you plan to make changes based on the suggestions they offer. This models reflective practice and ensures that any future feedback is thoughtful.

> **Lisa's thoughts…**
> At semester midterm I asked the students for their written feedback to the following questions: (1) share one suggestion that I could implement (as your teacher) in the next seven weeks to make these classes even better; and (2) share one suggestion that you could

implement (as a student or classmate) in the next seven weeks to make these classes even better. After reviewing the results, I responded to the students with the following email:

Dear Students,

Thank you for providing me with some suggestions to make our classes even BETTER in the next seven weeks. First of all, I would like to express my gratitude for the many kind words that I have received. I am thrilled that many of you are enjoying my course(s) and my teaching methods. This means a lot to me!

I have carefully read all of the suggestions that you have made and would like to address some of them that appeared most often. Unfortunately, I am unable to reduce the workload of assignments as I must ensure that we are meeting the program standards and learning outcomes. These learning outcomes are required to ensure that you have the skills needed in future semesters and in your field placement (sorry!). I do appreciate that many of you feel supported and guided with the many resources available to allow you to succeed.

I am able to implement the following suggestions that you have made in the following (last) seven weeks:

- *Providing my PowerPoint presentations on eCentennial would be helpful, especially to enlarge the font on some of the slides. I will attempt to do this for you starting in week 8. Remind me if I forget.*
- *Providing more group work in the classroom (without grades) by participating in group activities. I will try to increase group work activities moving forward. Some students requested that I assign groups (when grades are involved) in our next assignment involving group work to allow an opportunity to work with other students. Although we do not have any more group assignments in the Healthy Development, I can assign groups in the Learning Environment.*
- *Some students expressed how nervous they are feeling for the Healthy Development Midterm test since it makes up a high percentage of the final grade. They asked if I could send out a small sample of similar questions before the test so they can get a feel for the type of questions on the test. I will send out six sample questions by email before the test to everyone.*
- *A few students asked about assignment extension. Please remember that I sent out a memo at the beginning of our course that discusses how to get an extension on assignments if needed. Please review this memo if you have any further questions about extension.*
- *Lastly, many students want more cookies. OK, more cookies to come!*

Thank you for your comments. I hope that you feel that I have considered your suggestions and implemented them where possible. I also look forward to your contributions to making our final weeks the best that they can be!

Sincerely,
Lisa McCaie ☺

Once the students received my email, I received several emails of gratitude for being heard. Here is one example:

Hi Professor McCaie,
First of all, I just wanted to say thank you for the cards you sent me. I really do appreciate all the praise, encouragement, and support. You know, to be perfectly honest, you are one of the select few teachers I've had who truly cares for her students. I hate to admit it, but majority of the teachers I've had in all of my school years only teach simply because it's their job. You on the other hand are unique. You care for your student's successes. You are passionate about what you do. You are humble enough in that you ask your students to provide you with ideas on how to make your classroom and teaching better. You taught us a lot about active learning, but I think they should add a new word and it should be called, 'active teaching' because that is what you personify. You inspire a lot of people to want to learn. And trust me when I say, many people in your class feel the same way because I've talked with a lot of them. I was reading this book the other day called, "Teaching to Change Lives" by Dr. Howard Hendricks. In the book, there was a student who asked his teacher, "Why do you read so much?" And the teacher replied, "Son, I would rather have my students drink from a running stream than a stagnant pool." You are a lot like that teacher and for that I say, "Thank you for making your students drink from a running stream instead of a stagnant pool!" Have a great day and I'll see you next week!

Jenny's thoughts...
I have completed this type of paper evaluation in class, but this was the first time I uploaded it online. Students could provide anonymous responses. I found the feedback, much more detailed and honest. The one thing I have realized about 'ah ha' moments is that you have to have an open mind otherwise you might miss it.

I tend to be selective with the notes and handouts I post on eCentennial, as I want to encourage students to come to class. However, this comment challenged my perspective in a positive way.

> *"I would LOVE if you put more content on eCentennial. It is such a HUGE resource we have, and helpful when on the go to have the class slides on our device. I can study in the car, at the park even in the grocery checkout."*

Ironically, I was in the check out at the Superstore when I read this! This comment allowed me to truly see things from the student's point of view. As a reflective practitioner, accessing regular feedback from students can be a great opportunity to see things through a different lens.

Remember, you don't have to wait until midterm to collect student feedback. With some simple questions, you can check in with your students at the end of a class or after you have taught a particularly difficult concept. Use any of the following questions at the end of class (see below) or Paola Ostinelli's *Exit Ticket* (see below) to collect quick feedback and adjust your teaching plans for the next class.

Questions to Collect Feedback
1. What was the most important idea/insight from today's class?
2. What is the question that most needs addressing from today's class?
3. What was the most confusing idea from today's class?
4. What was the most poorly explained idea from today's class?
5. What was the most poorly demonstrated process from today's class?
6. What was the least clear idea or technique from today's class?

Paola's thoughts…
One example I use to gauge student's learning and retention in a class is an exit ticket. After a class, and before students leave, I give them a minute or two as they're packing up to quickly write out what stuck out for them - what they're leaving with for the class. I then have them stick their 'ticket' on a flip chart, and then I can review what students are retaining, what needs to be worked on, etc. This can also be flipped - they can write down a question they still have, or something they find confusing, which I can then address in the recap the following class.

Before you leave!

Exit ticket:

| The most important thing I learned today is... |

| What you learned in140 characters or less! #[course code] |

| What stuck for you today? |

What I learned is that my first-year students, who are more engaged in the class work, had constructive and realistic feedback around the 'Stop, Start, Continue.' In the fall semester I also created another exit ticket activity along the lines of 'what stuck with you'; I asked students to imagine they were creating a time capsule for that class, and we were all to record our most memorable piece of information from the class. Their replies were insightful and showed me that they met the learning objectives for the class, since they could demonstrate their learning in a quick snapshot.

Your Reflections

Upon completing this activity, reflect on your collecting and implementing feedback during the mid-way point of your course using the following questions as a guide:

1. What did you learn about yourself from this activity? What surprised you?

_____

_____

_____

2. What do you do well? (It is OK to congratulate yourself!)

_____

_____

_____

3. What change(s) would you like to consider right now? In the future?

_____

_____

_____

4. SoTL: How will this impact what you know, what you value, and how you will act (i.e., impact on your scholarly teaching and/or contributions to teaching and learning scholarship)?

_____

_____

_____

Sue Wells, Lisa McCaie, Megan Barker & Marilyn Herie

Teaching in the Digital World

At most community colleges, teaching has historically occurred within the four walls of a classroom, workplace, or laboratory. As colleges adapt to the complex demands on student's time and their comfort with technology, more and more learning is occurring online within asynchronous environments. As a faculty member teaching online classes, you have been tasked with creating an online learning environment that meets the same course standards and outcomes as a traditional classroom, without the ability to rely on your in-person facilitation tools. In doing so, you may find it more challenging to obtain 'in-the-moment' feedback from students within the digital learning space. How do you know if you are teaching effectively in the online environment? Is being an effective online teacher any different than being an effective classroom teacher?

Activity 9: Benchmark of Online Teaching Excellence

In this activity, you will create your own *Benchmark of Online Teaching Excellence* and use it as a tool for reflection. To begin, consider the question posed above: *is being an effective online teacher any different than being an effective classroom teacher?* Below you will find the criteria that were used in an earlier exercise, *Activity 6: Call A Friend.*

Step One: Identify Classroom Criteria

Review the list below and put a check mark beside any criteria that you feel are important components of the traditional (in-person) classroom.

Step Two: Identify Online Criteria

Repeat the exercise, placing a check mark beside any criteria that you think are important components of the online classroom.

	TEACHING SKILLS	**Classroom Teaching**	**Online Teaching**
A.	**IMPORTANCE AND SUITABILITY OF CONTENT**		
1.	The material covered is generally accepted by industry professionals/practitioners to be relevant	☐	☐
2.	The material is important for this group of students	☐	☐
3.	Students seem to have the necessary background to	☐	☐

	TEACHING SKILLS	**Classroom Teaching**	**Online Teaching**
	understand the class material		
4.	The examples used drew upon student's experiences	☐	☐
5.	When appropriate, a distinction was made between factual material and opinions	☐	☐
6.	When appropriate, references were cited to support assertions or to source content shared or presented	☐	☐
7.	Sufficient material was included in the class	☐	☐
8.	Content represents current thinking in the discipline	☐	☐
9.	Class material is relevant to course objectives and assigned readings, lab work, co-op or placement experience, etc.	☐	☐
B.	**ORGANIZATION OF CONTENT**		
	Introductory Portion		
1.	Stated purpose of the class	☐	☐
2.	Presented brief overview of the class content	☐	☐
3.	Stated a problem to be solved or discussed during the class	☐	☐
4.	Made explicit the relationship between today's and the previous class	☐	☐
	Body of Class		
1.	Arranged and discussed the content in a systematic and organized fashion that was made explicit to the students	☐	☐
2.	Asked questions periodically to determine whether too much or too little information was being presented	☐	☐
3.	Presented information at an appropriate level of abstraction	☐	☐
4.	Presented examples to clarify very abstract/difficult ideas	☐	☐
5.	Explicitly stated relationship among various ideas	☐	☐
6.	Periodically summarized the most important ideas in the class	☐	☐
7.	Provided a balance of at least 50% of classroom or lab time Spent in experiential learning (application and practice of knowledge and skills), relative to lecturing/presenting	☐	☐
	Conclusion of Class		
1.	Summarized the main ideas	☐	☐
2.	Solved or otherwise dealt with any problems that arose during the class	☐	☐
3.	Related the day's class to upcoming classes/events	☐	☐
4.	Restated what students were expected to gain from the class	☐	☐

TEACHING SKILLS		Classroom Teaching	Online Teaching
	material and how this will inform professional practice		
	Voice Characteristics		
1.	Rate of speech was neither too fast nor too slow	☐	☐
2.	Voice was raised or lowered for variety and emphasis	☐	☐
3.	Speech was neither too formal nor too casual	☐	☐
4.	Speech fillers, for example "okay?", "right", and "umm" were not distracting	☐	☐
5.	Rate of speech was neither too fast nor too slow	☐	☐
	Nonverbal Communication		
1.	Wasn't too casual in style	☐	☐
2.	Facial and body movements did not contradict speech or expressed intentions. For example, waited for responses after asking questions	☐	☐
3.	Used gestures effectively	☐	☐
	General Style		
1.	Demonstrated enthusiasm for subject matter	☐	☐
2.	Demonstrated command of subject matter	☐	☐
3.	Modeled professional and ethical behaviour	☐	☐
4.	Used instructional aids to communicate important points	☐	☐
C.	**CLARITY OF PRESENTATION**		
1.	Stated purpose at the beginning of the class	☐	☐
2.	Defined new terms, concepts, and principles	☐	☐
3.	Told the students why certain processes, techniques, or formulae were used to solve problems	☐	☐
4.	Used relevant examples to explain major ideas	☐	☐
5.	Used clear and simple examples	☐	☐
6.	Explicitly related new ideas to already familiar ones	☐	☐
7.	Reiterated definitions of new terms to help students become accustomed to them	☐	☐
8.	Provided occasional summaries and restatements of important ideas	☐	☐
9.	Used alternate explanations when necessary	☐	☐
10.	Slowed the word flow when ideas were complex and difficult	☐	☐

	TEACHING SKILLS	Classroom Teaching	Online Teaching
11.	Did not often digress from the main topic	☐	☐
12.	Spoke directly to the class	☐	☐
13.	If used, slides were professional, well-designed, impactful, engaging, referenced appropriately, and complemented spoken content	☐	☐
D.	**ASKING QUESTIONS**		
1.	About the class topic: asked questions to see what the students knew	☐	☐
2.	Addressed questions to individual students as well as group at large	☐	☐
3.	Paused after all questions to allow students time to think	☐	☐
4.	Encouraged students to answer difficult questions by providing cues or rephrasing	☐	☐
5.	When necessary, asked students to clarify their questions	☐	☐
6.	Asked probing questions if a student's answer was incomplete or superficial	☐	☐
7.	Repeated answers when necessary so the entire class could hear	☐	☐
8.	Received student's questions politely and, when possible, enthusiastically	☐	☐
9.	Refrained from answering questions when unsure of a correct response; offered to find the answer with students, or challenged students to find the answer	☐	☐
10.	Requested that very difficult, time-consuming questions of limited interest be discussed before or after class or during office hours	☐	☐
11.	Asked a variety of types of questions (rhetorical, open and closed)	☐	☐
12.	Addressed questions to volunteer and non-volunteer students	☐	☐
E.	**ESTABLISHING AND MAINTAINING CONTACT WITH STUDENTS**		
	Establishing Contact	☐	☐
1.	Greeted students with small talk	☐	☐
2.	Established eye contact with as many students as possible	☐	☐
3.	Set ground rules for student participation and questioning	☐	☐
4.	Used questions to gain student attention	☐	☐

	TEACHING SKILLS	**Classroom Teaching**	**Online Teaching**
5.	Encouraged student's questions and contributions	☐	☐
	Maintaining Contact		
1.	Maintained eye contact with as many students as possible	☐	☐
2.	Used rhetorical questions to re-engage student attention	☐	☐
3.	Asked questions which allowed the professor to gauge student progress	☐	☐
4.	Answered student's questions satisfactorily	☐	☐
5.	Noted and responded to signs of puzzlement, boredom, curiosity, and so on	☐	☐
6.	Varied the pace of the class to keep students alert	☐	☐
7.	Spoke at a rate which allowed students time to take notes	☐	☐

Step 3: Reflecting on Your Responses

Review the items that you have checked off in each column above and pause to reflect.

1. What did you learn about the similarities between effective teaching techniques for classroom and online learning environments?

   _____

   _____

   _____

2. What did you learn about the differences between effective teaching techniques for classroom and online learning environments?

   _____

   _____

   _____

3. How will you apply this learning to your own online learning environment?

   _____

   _____

   _____

Marah's thoughts…
One of the challenges I face when introducing the hybrid format to students is their initial reaction to online learning. Having seen a pattern every semester in their responses, I've endeavored to create an online learning environment that provides consistency. This is important because it helps students navigate their way without feeling lost or unsure. I gather feedback from students early in the semester asking questions such as:
- Was the layout easy to follow?
- Was the technology easy to use and did it work well?
- Did the presentation have the right amount of content?
- Was it easy to navigate the hyperlinks?

Step Four: Making your Online Classroom just as Amazing as your Face-to-Face Classroom
Despite the similarities and the differences between effective teaching strategies for classroom and online learning environments, there are some approaches that happen quite naturally in the face-to-face classroom, that require, at least initially, a little more consideration and creativity to replicate within an online learning environment. Generate a list of these items. What have you created in your traditional classroom that you would like to see replicated in an online classroom? Perhaps it is the personal connection with your students, rich student collaboration, or your storytelling. Identifying these approaches is the first step to ensuring your online learning environment is just as rich, meaningful and dynamic as your face-to-face classroom.

Marah's thoughts…
Developing a relationship with my students is one important objective that I strive to achieve. This is important because it helps the learning environment become a safe space to ask questions or share ideas. During the weeks that the students are online, I try to ensure my voice and personality are still present in the voice-over lectures and activities that I include. I think about each activity and reflect on its appropriateness to the week's content. An example is the use of quotes. I will select one quote and pose a question asking how the students feel about the quote. This is one way to get students to think about the week's topic.

Thoughts from the Child and Family Studies Department (C&FS) and Community Services Department (CS) at Centennial…
We entered a collaborative, iterative process to discover ways to enhance student's experiences within an online learning environment. Through research, experimentation, discovery and student feedback we created a list of items that we felt made high quality online learning. We then committed to this benchmark as a standard of practice for all online

course development. We believe that we can enhance the student experience of hybrid learning by attending to the following items:

- ☐ Socialize students to online classes prior to implementation
- ☐ Maintain an open dialogue with students to monitor and respond to their online experiences supporting the students to be successful
- ☐ Creative use of online tools to support student learning (e.g., using voice over presentations to infuse the 'story telling' aspect of teaching in the classroom)
- ☐ Embed a 'help' feature for both content and IT into every blended class
- ☐ Engage with the students during online content delivery
- ☐ Use common terminology (e.g., face-to-face to describe in class sessions to be consistent with *Class Climate*)
- ☐ Support conscious integration between online and face-to-face classes so there is a flow from one week to the next (i.e., both environments support each other).

We believe that we can enhance the student experience of online learning by designing content with the following things in mind:

- ☐ Use a standardized department format that is simple to follow
- ☐ Encapsulate all items students need for one class in one place
- ☐ Utilize tools for online learning that support the desired learning outcomes
- ☐ Utilize tools for online learning that engage students in the learning experiences, provide for student-to-student and student-to-faculty interaction, and are selected to meet the needs of diverse learners
- ☐ Provide a variety of tools for online learning while being sensitive to the student's learning of the tool itself, the number of different tools being used and the system requirements necessary to use each tool
- ☐ Integrate online and face-to-face learning activities into a coherent whole (i.e., both environments support one another)
- ☐ Infuse content with faculty voice and personality
- ☐ Provide learning experiences that match the academic rigor and time of the in-class experience.

Review the above lists as inspiration and check off the items that are important to you. What would you like to add to your own list?

_____

_____

_____

_____

_____

_____

Step Five: Creating Your Own Criteria

You will now create your own *Benchmark for Online Teaching Excellence*. Throughout the previous steps in this activity you have reviewed and identified the elements that foster teaching excellence within the face-to-face classroom and online learning environments, and reflected on similarities and differences between them. You then broadened this list to identify the elements that are important to your own teaching practice and would like to incorporate within your own online learning environment. You now have a comprehensive list of elements that you can use to create your personalized *Benchmark for Online Teaching Excellence*.

Review the items that you have checked off in the above sections and rank their level of importance. Use H for high importance, M for medium importance, and L for low importance. Don't deliberate for too long, trust you first instinct! Try to prioritize the use of "H" to ten items. Now use the items that you have ranked as "H" and create your own *Benchmark for Online Teaching Excellence* in the following chart.

My Benchmark for Online Teaching Excellence
1.
2.
3.
4.
5.
6.
7.
8.
9.
10.

Step Six: Put it into Action

Your personalized *Benchmark for Online Teaching Excellence* is now ready to be used as a tool for your reflective practice! Consider using it in one of the following ways:

1. Use it in private reflection as you prepare and review course curriculum.
2. Invite a faculty colleague for coffee and ask for their feedback on your *Benchmark for Online Teaching Excellence*.
3. Provide a colleague with access to your online courses and ask them to provide you with feedback on how well you have achieved your benchmarks.
4. With a simple adaption to a survey tool, invite your students to provide you with feedback regarding how well you have achieved your benchmarks.

Your Reflections

Upon completing this activity, reflect on what it was like creating your own *Benchmark for Online Teaching Excellence* using the following questions as a guide:

1. What did you learn about yourself from this activity? What surprised you?

_____
_____
_____

2. What do you do well? (It is OK to congratulate yourself!)

_____
_____
_____

3. What change(s) would you like to consider right now? In the future?

_____
_____
_____

4. SoTL: How will this impact what you know, what you value, and how you will act (i.e., impact on your scholarly teaching and/or contributions to teaching and learning scholarship)?

_____
_____
_____

Sue Wells, Lisa McCaie, Megan Barker & Marilyn Herie

Creating a Safe Space for Learning

Determining class outcomes, scaffolding content to foster student learning, creating clear visual supports, designing engaging activities – these are just a few of the tasks you are responsible for as you plan each class. However, it is equally important that you also establish a safe space to support learning for all students. An environment where students feel included, welcomed, and respected provides a space where they can focus on learning new ideas and concepts. With the diversity that students bring to the classroom, it is no easy task to facilitate this environment. It takes thoughtful, intentional, and ongoing actions on your part to ensure you are meeting your student's needs. How then do you know if you are successful in creating an inclusive classroom?

Activity 10: Is Your Classroom Welcoming and Safe?

Faculty in department of Child and Family Studies (CF&S) at Centennial College have spent some time considering if their classrooms feel welcoming and safe to all students. In this activity, you will consider the strategies that faculty in C&FS have implemented to create welcome and safe spaces for students to learn. Take a moment and identify which strategies you use.

Do you…?	Response	Example/Comments
Create classroom 'ground rules' with students at the start of each course where mutual guidelines for discussion and debate are outlined? Do you refer to these guidelines throughout the course particularly when contentious discussion topics are planned for the class?	☐ Yes ☐ No	
Learn each student's name (and how to pronounce it)?	☐ Yes ☐ No	
Respectfully address microaggressions, misconceptions or stereotypical comments that occur in class?	☐ Yes ☐ No	

Create opportunities for students to share their uniqueness?	☐ Yes ☐ No	
Use vigilance when choosing pictures, videos, textbooks, etc. to ensure a balance of perspectives and images reflective of the students in your classroom and beyond?	☐ Yes ☐ No	
Monitor your own biases and assumptions and their impact on teaching and student interactions?	☐ Yes ☐ No	
Challenge students to critically reflect on their own biases, assumptions, worldviews and standpoints?	☐ Yes ☐ No	
Explicitly affirm and model principles of equity and inclusion in how you interact with students?	☐ Yes ☐ No	
Provide closure and/or follow-up when there is a difficult classroom discussion where students express contentious points of view?	☐ Yes ☐ No	
Learn about, understand, and provide compassion regarding the life experiences of your students while still maintaining clear and consistent academic standards?	☐ Yes ☐ No	

What other activities are you doing that are not listed above, yet you feel contribute to creating a welcome and safe classroom environment?

_____

_____

_____

_____
_____
_____

Review your answers to the above checklist and congratulate yourself on those that you are already implementing. These are the actions that you can take to ensure your students feel valued and respected during their time at college. Also pause to consider those points for which you replied 'no', or those for which you hesitated before answering. Is there a practice you would like to try in your next class? Consider what you would like to change and record it in the table below:

Date of Implementation:	
Strategies I will try:	
Outcomes and implications for my learning and development:	

Your Reflections

Upon completing this activity, reflect on what it was like to explore inclusivity in your classroom using the following questions as a guide:

1. What did you learn about yourself from this activity? What surprised you?

_____
_____
_____

2. What do you do well? (It is OK to congratulate yourself!)

_____

_____

_____

3. What change(s) would you like to consider right now? In the future?

_____

_____

_____

4. SoTL: How will this impact what you know, what you value, and how you will act (i.e., impact on your scholarly teaching and/or contributions to teaching and learning scholarship)?

_____

_____

_____

Ask the Students

Your students have unique perspective on your teaching abilities. Giving them an opportunity to voice their perspectives, opinions, and experiences can provide you with powerful feedback for self-reflection. Student feedback surveys and questionnaires are useful, but an actual conversation with students provides data that is rich and more in-depth than what they can provide in a written format. Discussion provides the opportunity to clarify questions, create synergy among those involved, follow-up on unclear responses, and offer suggestions. The resulting data is useful information to inform next steps.

Activity 11: Student Focus Group

In this activity, you will collect qualitative data through a student focus group. Follow these guidelines to make your student focus group a success.

Step One: Identify a Facilitator

Recruit someone to host your student focus group. It is critical that you choose someone who does not have a relationship with your students in another context (e.g., teaches, evaluates, or advises them). Pick someone who can facilitate the students' discussion, providing an opportunity for everyone to speak, while probing for additional clarification as required. It would be ideal to have a note taker as well. This person can take notes during the conversation and summarize them afterwards to identify themes and provide quotes. If a note taker is not available, the facilitator should also assume this role.

Step Two: Focus the Focus Group

Decide on the areas of your teaching where you would like feedback. Consider the following ideas:

- Planning: Does the course flow? Do students know where you are going (i.e., class outcomes, course learning outcomes)?
- Assessments: Have they been clear? Do they understand assessment criteria? Has it been fair? Has feedback been timely and helpful?
- Online and Face-to-Face Teaching: Are you clear when you teach concepts? Are you engaging? Are your teaching techniques effective?
- Out of Class Assistance: Is it available? Is it helpful?
- Online Learning Environments: Are the content and activities clear? Are they engaging? Is it connected to a face-to-face class?

Step Three: Create the Questions

For the best results, create questions that are open-ended and solicit opinions, perceptions or suggestions from the students. Arrange in a logical order (general to more specific). Limit yourself to 7-8 questions for a one hour focus group.

Step Four: Find the Students

There really is no right or wrong group of students to select for participation in the focus group. All students will provide a unique perspective and with it, valuable insight for your reflection. Aim for a group of about ten students. Remember to explain your reasons for the focus group, remind them that confidentiality will be assured, and follow-up by sharing the results. Offering pizza can always be guaranteed to increase participation!

Be aware that selecting and inviting students may result in others feeling left out and/or undervalued. Providing an opportunity for students to volunteer and then holding a random draw if the group is too large may mitigate this risk.

Step Five: Reflect on the Results

Once the data is collected, reflect on the feedback by considering the following questions:

1. What student feedback surprised you or challenged your perception?

_____
_____
_____

2. What student feedback did you expect to hear, but did not?

_____
_____
_____

3. What teaching strength was affirmed by the student feedback?

_____
_____
_____

4. What changes would you like make to your teaching because of your student's feedback?

_____

_____

_____

5. What is one action that you would like to implement immediately because of this feedback?

_____

_____

_____

Your Reflections

Upon completing this activity, reflect on what it was like to offer a student focus group and receive feedback using the following questions as a guide:

1. What did you learn about yourself from this activity? What surprised you?

_____

_____

_____

2. What do you do well? (It is OK to congratulate yourself!)

_____

_____

_____

3. What change(s) would you like to consider right now? In the future?

_____

_____

_____

4. SoTL: How will this impact what you know, what you value, and how you will act (i.e., impact on your scholarly teaching and/or contributions to teaching and learning scholarship)?

_____

_____

_____

Advancing Academic Integrity

The Centennial College *Academic Honesty Policy and Procedures* outlines the range of possible breaches of academic integrity, as well as potential sanctions. All students are expected to familiarize themselves with this important policy. In addition, faculty and administrators are charged with implementing the policy and following academic integrity procedures when breaches occur. However, students, faculty, and administrators alike all struggle with academic integrity for a variety of reasons. From the students' perspective, they may not understand or be familiar with institutional academic integrity policies and procedures, or may willfully ignore them. For faculty and academic administrators, responses to student breaches of academic integrity may not always be applied consistently across courses, programs, departments, and schools. And from a faculty perspective, how do you know that your response to a student breach is the right one?

As you review the guidelines and recommendations below, consider how they compare with your own approach to addressing academic integrity breaches with students. The guidelines and recommendations were arrived at using a consensus panel approach, and it should be noted that they are just that: *guidelines*. Flexibility and care are required when working with individual student situations. Nonetheless, the process of critically reflecting on how we respond to incidents of academic dishonesty, and coming up with a more consistent approach, provides a stronger foundation for your decision-making.

Faculty Role in Responding to Academic Integrity Breaches

Consider student concerns you have dealt with relating to academic integrity. There is a range of responses, from more lenient to more severe, and this depends on numerous factors. This is complex, high-stakes decision-making, for the student as well as the reputation and integrity of the college itself. Although the final decision regarding sanctions for offences for a student breach of academic integrity lies with the Chairperson, faculty play a role in recommending the sanction for consideration.

How do the following considerations resonate for you as you consider how to respond when faced with a student breach of academic integrity?

- Apply sanction depending on the context and severity of the offense (e.g., extent of copying or plagiarism/cheating).
- Also determine the type of sanction based on the semester in which the student is enrolled (e.g., first semester versus upper semester).

- Consider the type of program: post-grad students would be presumed to better know the academic integrity policy and implications for practice.
- Consider premeditation to also inform severity of the penalty.
- Examine the assignment itself for clarity of instructions and other possible deficiencies in the design of the assessment that may contribute to academic dishonesty.

Note: It is strongly recommended that all academic integrity offences, without exception, are documented and held on file in the Office of the Dean of the home School.

In all cases, breaches of academic dishonesty, and the consequences to students, represent an important and meaningful "teachable moment" relating to honesty and integrity more broadly: in academic, occupational and personal contexts and settings. Consider framing the conversation with the student as a learning opportunity, including the consequences to the student and how this will impact their approach as professionals in training going forward.

Activity 12: Academic Integrity Sanctions: How Do You Compare?

Review the list below[2] and reflect on the sanction that you would impose or recommend for each of the possible offenses. How do you compare with these guidelines? What questions does this raise for you to bring to your faculty colleagues/team or Chairperson?

Part 1: Cheating

1. Copying from another student or permitting another student to copy material

Recommended Sanction(s)		
First Offence	**Second Offence**	**Notes**
☐ Verbal warning – breach of academic honesty form completed ☐ Lower grade on assignment/test	☐ F grade on assignment/test ☐ F grade in the course	

[2] The list provided has been generated from the *Centennial College Consensus Panel Recommendations: Responding to Student Breaches of Academic Integrity*

2. Consulting an unauthorized source during an evaluation

Recommended Sanction(s)		
First Offence	**Second Offence**	**Notes**
☐ Verbal warning – breach of academic honesty form completed ☐ Lower grade on assignment/test ☐ F grade on assignment/test	☐ F grade on assignment/test ☐ F in course	

3. Using unauthorized aids or materials during an evaluation

Recommended Sanction(s)		
First Offence	**Second Offence**	**Notes**
☐ Verbal warning – breach of academic honesty form completed ☐ Lower grade on assignment/test ☐ F grade on assignment/test	☐ F grade on assignment/test ☐ F in course	

4. Obtaining a copy of an examination or test in advance of the date and time for writing the examination or test

Recommended Sanction(s)		
First Offence	**Second Offence**	**Notes**
☐ F grade on assignment/test ☐ F in course ☐ F in course with permanent record of grade on transcript ☐ Notation on transcript: six months	☐ F grade on assignment/test ☐ F in course ☐ F in course with permanent record of grade on transcript ☐ Notation on transcript: six months ☐ Notation on transcript: one year ☐ Recommend suspension	If the copy of the test answers are actively sought out or stolen by the student (as opposed to opportunistic access), more severe sanctions would be imposed especially for a second offense.

5. Submitting the work one has done for one class or project to a second class, or as a second project, without the prior consent of the faculty member receiving the assignment

Recommended Sanction(s)		
First Offence	**Second Offence**	**Notes**
☐ Lower grade on assignment/test (see notes)	☐ F grade on assignment/test ☐ F in course	Of all offenses, this is may be one of the least likely to be known by students to constitute an offense. Depending on the student context, may permit the student to rewrite the assignment with a maximum C grade on the assignment.

6. Submitting work prepared in collaboration with another member(s) of a class, when collaborative work on a project has not been authorized by the faculty member

Recommended Sanction(s)		
First Offence	**Second Offence**	**Notes**
☐ Verbal warning – breach of academic honesty form completed ☐ Lower grade on assignment/test ☐ F grade on assignment/test	☐ F in course	Range of sanctions for first offense based on the extent of unauthorized collaboration and/or duplication of assignment content. May also permit student to revise and resubmit assignment for a lower grade (first offense).

7. Submitting work prepared in whole or in part by another person or source and representing that work as one's own

Recommended Sanction(s)		
First Offence	**Second Offence**	**Notes**
☐ Verbal warning – breach of academic honesty form completed ☐ Lower grade on assignment/test ☐ F grade on assignment/test	☐ F grade on assignment/test ☐ F in course	Mindful that some students are not taught APA/correct citation until later in their academic program. Consider *not* penalizing students for improper formatting of citations versus not citing sources used in the assignment.

8. Offering for sale essays or other assignments, in whole or in part, with the expectation that these works will be submitted by a student for appraisal

Recommended Sanction(s)		
First Offence	**Second Offence**	**Notes**
☐ Notation on transcript: six months ☐ Notation on transcript: one year	☐ Notation on transcript: six months ☐ Notation on transcript: one year ☐ Suspension ☐ Expulsion	This offense is also related to the Student Code of Conduct, as this may involve two students enrolled in different courses. If students are in the same course, they would receive an academic penalty. If in a different course or selling essays/assignments from a previous course, consider a notation on the student transcript. Refer student for follow up sanctions under the Student Code of Conduct Policy.

9. Preparing work in whole or in part, with the expectation that this work will be submitted by another student for appraisal.

Recommended Sanction(s)		
First Offence	**Second Offence**	**Notes**
☐ Notation on transcript: six months ☐ Notation on transcript: one year	☐ Notation on transcript: six months ☐ Notation on transcript: one year ☐ Suspension	This offense also relates to the Student Code of Conduct, as this situation could involve two students enrolled in different courses. If in a different course or selling essays/assignments from a previous course, recommended to impose a notation on the student transcript. Refer student for follow up sanctions under the Student Code of Conduct Policy.

Part 2: Plagiarism

To present another person's ideas, writing, artistic work, creations, etc. as one's own.

Recommended Sanction(s)		
First Offence	**Second Offence**	**Notes**
☐ Verbal warning – breach of academic honesty form completed ☐ Lower grade on assignment/test ☐ F grade on assignment/test ☐ F in course	☐ F grade on assignment/test ☐ F in course	Depending on the extent of plagiarism (e.g., one paragraph versus the entire document).

Part 3: Impersonation

To have someone impersonate oneself in class, in a test, examination or interview, or at any stage in the admission process, or in connection with any other type of assignment or placement associated with a course or academic program (refers to both the impersonator and the individual impersonated).

Recommended Sanction(s)		
First Offence	**Second Offence**	**Notes**
☐ F in course ☐ Notation on transcript: six months ☐ Notation on transcript: one year ☐ Suspension	☐ F in course with permanent record of grade on transcript ☐ Notation on transcript: six months ☐ Notation on transcript: one year ☐ Suspension ☐ Expulsion	

Part 4: Falsification

Falsification, fabrication, or modification of an application, supporting documentation, assignment, etc. To falsify, fabricate or in any way modify, either through omission or commission, an application and supporting documentation to the College and any of its departments.

Recommended Sanction(s)		
First Offence	**Second Offence**	**Notes**
☐ F in course ☐ Notation on transcript: six months ☐ Notation on transcript: one year ☐ Suspension	☐ F in course with permanent record of grade on transcript ☐ Notation on transcript: six months ☐ Notation on transcript: one year ☐ Suspension ☐ Expulsion	If falsification of documents are not related to student course (e.g., falsification of Police Check, Doctor's note), then refer to Student Code of Conduct Policy.

Part 5: Aiding and Abetting

To encourage, enable or cause others to do or attempt any of the above with intent to mislead a faculty member, academic unit, program, office or committee as to a student's academic status, qualifications, actions or preparation, or knowingly assisting anyone in a breach of academic honesty.

Recommended Sanction(s)		
First Offence	**Second Offence**	**Notes**
☐ F grade on assignment/test ☐ F in course ☐ F in course with permanent record of grade on transcript ☐ Notation on transcript: six months ☐ Notation on transcript: one year ☐ Suspension	☐ F in course ☐ F in course with permanent record of grade on transcript ☐ Notation on transcript: six months ☐ Notation on transcript: one year ☐ Suspension	If not related to student's course (e.g. falsification of a Police Check, Doctor's note), then refer to Student Code of Conduct Policy.

Part 6: Inappropriate Use of Computer Technology

To use another person's identification and/or password, or unauthorized entry into a computer file for the purpose of using, reading, changing or deleting its contents, or the unauthorized transfer in whole or part of files for academic gain.

Recommended Sanction(s)		
First Offence	**Second Offence**	**Notes**
☐ F in course ☐ F in course with permanent record of grade on transcript ☐ Notation on transcript: six months ☐ Notation on transcript: one year ☐ Suspension	☐ F in course ☐ F in course with permanent record of grade on transcript ☐ Notation on transcript: six months ☐ Notation on transcript: one year ☐ Suspension ☐ Expulsion	If not related to student's course, then refer to Student Code of Conduct Policy.

Part 7: Unauthorized Removal, Defacing, and Destruction of Materials from the Learning Resource Centres/Related Facilities

Depriving other students of academic resources is considered a breach of academic honesty.

Recommended Sanction(s)		
First Offence	**Second Offence**	**Notes**
☐ Notation on transcript: six months	☐ Notation on transcript: one year ☐ Suspension ☐ Expulsion	

Your Reflections

Upon completing this activity, reflect on what it was like generate and/or recommend sanctions for offenses as they relate to academic integrity using the following questions as a guide:

1. What did you learn about yourself from this activity? What surprised you?

_____

_____

_____

2. What do you do well? (It is OK to congratulate yourself!)

_____

_____

_____

3. What change(s) would you like to consider right now? In the future?

_____

_____

_____

4. SoTL: How will this impact what you know, what you value, and how you will act (i.e., impact on your scholarly teaching and/or contributions to teaching and learning scholarship)?

_____

_____

_____

Part 3: An Even Deeper Dive – Beyond Teaching

"Self-reflection is the school of wisdom."

- Baltasar Gracian

In this section, you will move beyond your role as a teacher and explore the other roles you fulfill as a faculty member. This section will help you to reflect on the full scope of what it means to be a faculty member through the following activities:

- What is Your Ideal Faculty Self, Beyond Teaching
- Call an Expert
- How Did That Meeting Go?
- Rating Your Leadership Competency
- Call Another Friend
- A Word with the Boss
- Managing Your Classroom
- Diversity in Curriculum and Teaching Practice
- Assessing Inclusive Pedagogy
- How Careful Are You?

Multiple opportunities for reflection and planning will be incorporated throughout this section to support you in striving for excellence in all aspects of your work.

Data Collection Tools: Focusing Beyond Teaching

Although the priority focus of your role is teaching, there are a myriad of other roles you play as a faculty member. These additional responsibilities play a vital role in fostering a high-quality learning experience for your students. Take a moment to think about the responsibilities that may form part of your role as a faculty member:

- ☐ Course-specific academic advising
- ☐ Supporting or recommending retention strategies
- ☐ Designing assessments
- ☐ Developing and revising courses
- ☐ Designing curriculum
- ☐ Designing and implementing student success strategies

- ☐ Participating in committees
- ☐ Participating in faculty meetings
- ☐ Research and Scholarship
- ☐ Preparing for accreditation
- ☐ Coaching/supporting faculty colleagues
- ☐ Supporting student recruitment or orientation

☐ Establishing linkages with industry partners/professionals

☐ Engaging in continuing professional development

☐ Developing new courses or programs

☐ Leading or participating in quality review processes

☐ Leading or participating in co-curricular activities with students

☐ Engaging in faculty-led international programs (FLIPs) or Global Citizenship and Equity Learning Experiences (GCELEs)

☐ Other _____

☐ Other_____

Upon reviewing these roles, it is easy to see how they have an impact on the quality of academic programs and the learning experience for students. From critical thinking to interpersonal skills, these roles require a broad and varied skill set, which may or may not be the same skills required to be an effective teacher. Your success and value as a faculty member, also requires you to be effective in these roles. These roles also provide another opportunity for reflective practice.

Activity 13: What is Your Ideal Faculty Self, Beyond Teaching

In *Part One* of this manual, you identified the values that you bring to your teaching practice. This was essential to provide a strong foundation and reference point to guide your reflective practice as it related to teaching. Equally important is the consideration of the values that guide the other roles you play beyond teaching.

What is your *Ideal Faculty Self* when you are in these complementary roles? What are the top five values that are most important to you? Reconsider the values in the list below from this perspective. Select the words that resonate the most with you, and/or add other words that fit with your goals. Check off as many as you like. Then, take a second look at the items you identified, and circle the top five values that are most important to you. Although these words will guide your reflective practice, don't think about them for too long. Pick the first ones that come to mind!

What are the top five values that are most important to your other faculty roles beyond teaching?

☐ Quality
☐ Honesty
☐ Achievement

☐ Respect
☐ Service
☐ Stewardship

☐ Autonomy
☐ Integrity
☐ Involvement

☐ Empowerment   ☐ Wisdom   ☐ Objectivity
☐ Balance   ☐ Inclusion   ☐ Openness
☐ Competence   ☐ Authenticity   ☐ Influence
☐ Commitment   ☐ Reliability   ☐ Accountability
☐ Courage   ☐ Teamwork   ☐ Passionate
☐ Cooperation   ☐ Advocacy   ☐ Learning-centered
☐ Creativity   ☐ Curiosity   ☐ Transformative
☐ Discipline   ☐ Acceptance   ☐ Equitable
☐ Flexibility   ☐ Balance   ☐ Ethical
☐ Integrity   ☐ Inspirational   ☐ Agile
☐ Perseverance   ☐ Compassion   ☐ Collaborative
☐ Order   ☐ Innovation   ☐ Accessible
☐ Other _____   ☐ Other _____   ☐ Other _____
☐ Other _____   ☐ Other _____   ☐ Other _____

Now that you have identified the core values that inform your actions and contributions in these complementary roles, write a definition for each of the words that you selected. Think more about what these values mean to you.

Using the lines below, write down your top core values and provide a short definition for each value:

1. _____
   _____
   _____

2. _____
   _____
   _____

3. _____
   _____
   _____

4. _____

_____

_____

5. _____

_____

_____

Think about your experience defining your values using the following questions as a guide:

1. How difficult or easy was it for you to define your foundational values as they relate to your non-teaching roles?

_____

_____

_____

2. Revisit the values you chose to define your teaching practice. Are they the same as those that define your other roles as a faculty member or are they different? What do these values reveal to you about the faculty member you would aspire to be?

_____

_____

_____

3. Our values inform how we see ourselves. Our collective charge is to act in ways that represent these values every day so that they shine through to those around us. If we can succeed at this, we model a powerful ethic of integrity to others. This modelling, in turn, supports our teams and our students in doing the same. How will you demonstrate your values as you engage in your non-teaching roles?

_____

_____

_____

4. How can you use your values to establish your personal signature as a faculty member?

_____

_____

_____

Data Collection Tools to Take an Even Deeper Dive

You have identified the work that you do 'beyond teaching' and reflected on the values that are important to you as you do this work. This section provides you with a sampling of tools that you can use to take an even 'deeper dive' and collect data on your effectiveness as a faculty member in the roles that you engage in beyond teaching. This data will help you to reflect on what you are doing, how well you are doing it, and how you might improve.

These data collection tools are not meant to be used in sequence or all at one time. Select one or two tools that resonate with you right now and return periodically to this section of the manual to try something new.

If you are interested in how others see your values in action, refer to *Activity 4: Cross Check* found in *Part Two* of this manual. This will guide you through a process to gather information from your students, your colleagues, and your Chairperson, revealing what their perspectives are.

Curriculum Design

Designing curriculum can be a sophisticated and complex process. The process involves developing a streamlined course that guides students along various milestones with the end goal of achieving specific learning outcomes. Curriculum design requires considerable skill in analysis, critical thinking, and knowledge of current content, combined with plenty of ingenuity and creativity. With so much skill and time involved in designing curriculum, how do you know if you are doing it well?

Activity 14: Call an Expert

In this activity, you will consult with a subject matter expert who will review and provide you with feedback on one of your courses or a series of courses connected to a broader program learning outcome. This person may be a skilled teacher or an industry expert in the content of your course or courses that you would like reviewed.

Consider the experience and strengths of the person you approach and your ultimate goal. If you want to know if your content is up-to-date, consider approaching a member of the Program Advisory Committee or a leader in your industry. Also, consider the value of asking a faculty member from another discipline to review your course(s). They can provide valuable insight to the structure and clarity of the content that you have created. Arrange a time to meet, provide the course outline(s) prior to the meeting, and let them know you would like to receive open and honest feedback as part of your reflective practice.

You may want to ask for feedback using (or adapting from) the following questions. You do not have to include all of these questions. They have been provided as a menu from which you can pick and choose.

1. Does the weekly progression create a clear pathway to the course learning outcomes?
2. Does the weighting of each topic and/or assessment align with the course learning outcomes?
3. Is the content up-to-date and reflective of current knowledge and practice?
4. Is there a clear relationship between applied/experiential learning activities and student assessment strategies?
5. Does the course design and learning activities meet the learning styles of a diversity of learners?
6. Is the course being taught to facilitate the appropriate level of learning for the required outcomes?
7. Does the design of the course and the learning activities engage the learner?
8. To what extent does the curriculum integrate diverse ways of knowing, being and doing, including Indigenous and global world views and perspectives/knowledge?
9. Does the curriculum integrate experiential and/or work-integrated learning opportunities?
10. Does the curriculum integrate principles of universal design for learning (UDL)?
11. Do the applied/experiential learning activities foster critical reflection, teamwork and collaboration (New Essential Skills, NES)?
12. Does the curriculum foster students' acquisition of innovation and entrepreneurship skills and capabilities (NES)?
13. Are there opportunities to shift lesson plans from a transmission (e.g. lecture style) delivery to a more constructivist, learner-centered and applied practice approach?

Your Reflections

Upon completing this activity, reflect on what it was like to receive feedback on your curriculum design skills by your colleagues and/or subject matter experts using the following questions as a guide:

1. What did you learn about yourself from this activity? What surprised you?

_____

_____

_____

2.   What do you do well? (It is OK to congratulate yourself!)

_____

_____

_____

3.   What change(s) would you like to consider right now? In the future?

_____

_____

_____

4.   SoTL: How will this impact what you know, what you value, and how you will act (i.e., impact on your scholarly teaching and/or contributions to teaching and learning scholarship)?

_____

_____

_____

Your Role as a Team Member

Although teaching often occurs in isolation from your colleagues, many of the other roles that you play as a faculty member will occur within teams. Faculty meetings, curriculum development teams or committee work, all involve team meetings where varying personalities and opinions will intersect. It can be challenging to ensure that your perspective, as well as your colleagues' points of view, are heard and considered. It is important that the professional expertise of each team member is respected and valued. With that being said, how are you viewed by others in your team meetings?

Activity 15: How Did That Meeting Go?

In this activity, you will invite a fellow team member to provide you with feedback. This person could be someone that facilitates your team meetings or a peer whose opinions you respect and value. Arrange a time to meet and let them know that you would like to receive open and honest feedback as part of your reflective practice.

If it feels uncomfortable to ask a fellow team member then consider the following options. You could ask a colleague outside of your team to join one of your meetings and provide their perspective or ask a colleague outside of your team to interview your fellow team members, collect feedback, and share the results with you.

You may want to ask for feedback using (or adapting from) the following questions. You do not have to include all of these questions. They have been provided as a menu from which you can pick and choose.

1. Do I speak too much in the meeting or not enough?
2. Am I prepared for the meeting?
3. Are my comments at the meeting valuable contributions to the discussion?
4. Do I introduce new ideas and/or provide critique or alternative perspectives in a respectful way?
5. Do I show respect for the opinions of others?
6. Do I support keeping the agenda on track and on time?
7. Do I offer new insights in an effective way? How so?
8. What should I start doing?
9. What should I stop doing?
10. To what extent do I embrace change and support the College in reaching its strategic goals and objectives?
11. Do I keep students front-and-centre throughout team discussions, consultations and/or decision-making?

Your Reflections

Upon completing this activity, reflect on what it was like to receive feedback from a peer on your role as a team member using the following questions as a guide:

1. What did you learn about yourself from this activity? What surprised you?

_____
_____
_____

2. What do you do well? (It is OK to congratulate yourself!)

_____
_____
_____

3. What change(s) would you like to consider right now? In the future?

_____

_____

_____

4. SoTL: How will this impact what you know, what you value, and how you will act (i.e., impact on your scholarly teaching and/or contributions to teaching and learning scholarship)?

_____

_____

_____

Leadership

A Chairperson provides leadership to a department to support the achievement of strategic directions, oversees the academic quality of programs within a department, contributes to committees to support project goals, and ensures faculty and staff act in accordance with college policies and procedures. However, Chairpersons are not the only leaders in a department. As a faculty member, you often assume the role of an academic leader within your department as you innovate, inspire creativity, cultivate critical relationships, model agility, plan for the future, and model leadership in a diverse and global environment. True leadership can be transformational to not only yourself and those around you, but your organization as a whole. Leadership is about being brave without bravado, a risk-taker without being risky, and a collaborator while maintaining independence.

Centennial College has developed a faculty leadership model that situates faculty members as, first and foremost, academic leaders. As a faculty member, your primary areas of focus (teaching excellence, academic quality and student success) represent dynamic, reciprocal and overlapping domains. Teaching excellence is insufficient without quality curricula (academic quality). Similarly, high-quality curriculum and teaching are designed to support students' success: engagement, persistence and preparedness for 'meaningful work and meaningful lives'.

Academic leadership occurs in an institutional context characterized by professional values and ethics, within a climate of respect, service and compassion where multiple ways of knowing and being are affirmed and valued. Collaboration with students, community and industry, and an emphasis on internationalization, indigenization, global citizenship and equity inform authentic and inclusive approaches to teaching and learning. This broader context also includes ongoing reflective practice, where creativity, inquiry and accountability foster continuing innovation.

Figure 5: Centennial College Academic Leadership Model

Activity 16: Rating Your Leadership Competencies

This activity will provide you with the opportunity to personally reflect on your leadership skills. The tool provided below is used as part of Centennial's Employee Leadership Passport self-assessment and has been adapted with permission from a tool developed at Algonquin College. Although it was developed as a self-reflection tool, it could easily be adapted and used to gather feedback on your leadership skills.

The tool consists of a series of items rated on a Likert scale and grouped under seven general leadership competencies. The survey takes approximately 15 minutes to complete. These competencies are mapped to the Leadership Framework for College Administrators (see Figure 6 below), but are also applicable and relevant to faculty members.

Figure 6: Cross-College Leadership Competencies

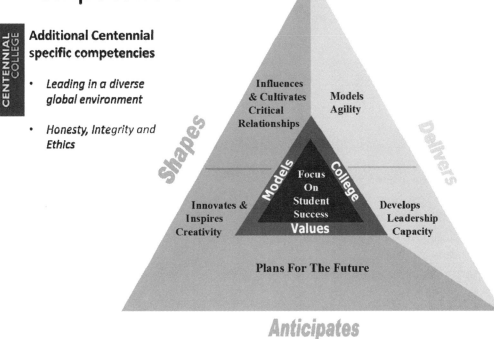

Thinking about your own teaching practice and various faculty roles, rate your leadership competencies using the tool below:

> **Innovate & Inspire Creativity**
> Champions innovation and continuous improvement by challenging the status quo, presenting new approaches, ideas and solutions, and encouraging others to do the same. Maintains a supportive environment to develop and implement new approaches effectively balancing risk-taking and return on investment.

To what extent do I/am I comfortable with or confident in my ability to…	1-Never	2-Very Rarely	3-Rarely	4-Occasionally	5-Frequently	6-Always
1. Sharing new knowledge, ideas, and opinions and ensure others have access to information	☐	☐	☐	☐	☐	☐

	1-Never	2-Very Rarely	3-Rarely	4-Occasionally	5-Frequently	6-Always
2. Promoting an environment that nurtures innovation across teams and encourages and supports professional development	☐	☐	☐	☐	☐	☐
3. Creating a climate for exchange and collaboration internally	☐	☐	☐	☐	☐	☐
4. Staying abreast of emerging industry and market trends	☐	☐	☐	☐	☐	☐
5. Challenging current thinking and drive continuous improvement	☐	☐	☐	☐	☐	☐
6. Fostering innovation and demonstrate a willingness to take calculated risks and learn from mistakes	☐	☐	☐	☐	☐	☐
7. Encouraging/empowering others to make innovative decisions	☐	☐	☐	☐	☐	☐
8. Looking for new ways to leverage technology to deliver programs and/or services	☐	☐	☐	☐	☐	☐
Influence & Cultivate Critical Relationships Builds effective and influential working relationships (internally and externally) and collaborates to achieve mutually beneficial goals.						
1. Fostering team spirit and promote high team performance	☐	☐	☐	☐	☐	☐
2. Maintaining a deep network of external contacts and encouraging others to	☐	☐	☐	☐	☐	☐

	1-Never	2-Very Rarely	3-Rarely	4-Occasionally	5-Frequently	6-Always
maintain and develop their own network						
3. Developing cross-department relationships	☐	☐	☐	☐	☐	☐
4. Modeling open two-way communications between teams and individuals	☐	☐	☐	☐	☐	☐
5. Engaging appropriate resources to make timely and effective decisions to execute plans	☐	☐	☐	☐	☐	☐
6. Involving the right people in making decisions, and leverage relationships and resources to get things done across the organization	☐	☐	☐	☐	☐	☐

Model Agility

Demonstrates both the focus and flexibility necessary to lead self and others during continuous change and ambiguity, while delivering results and maintaining exceptional levels of service to students.

	1-Never	2-Very Rarely	3-Rarely	4-Occasionally	5-Frequently	6-Always
1. Accurately appraise the strengths and weaknesses of individuals in the teams that I lead or participate in	☐	☐	☐	☐	☐	☐
2. Seek supervision and coaching when unsure about decisions or ambiguous situations	☐	☐	☐	☐	☐	☐
3. Balance multiple, competing priorities	☐	☐	☐	☐	☐	☐
4. Always perform my role with the student in mind	☐	☐	☐	☐	☐	☐
5. Reinforce change messages across teams and help others adapt to different ways of doing business	☐	☐	☐	☐	☐	☐
6. Reassess priorities in response to additional requests and new initiatives	☐	☐	☐	☐	☐	☐
7. Show an ability to balance the important with the urgent	☐	☐	☐	☐	☐	☐

	1-Never	2-Very Rarely	3-Rarely	4-Occasionally	5-Frequently	6-Always
8. Instill a sense of urgency for achieving departmental/team results	☐	☐	☐	☐	☐	☐
9. Apply focus and discipline to ensure objectives are achieved	☐	☐	☐	☐	☐	☐
10. Hold teams and individuals accountable for achieving performance goals	☐	☐	☐	☐	☐	☐

Develop Leadership Capacity
Identifies and actively develops the leadership talent necessary to realize the College's vision and successfully execute its strategy.

	1-Never	2-Very Rarely	3-Rarely	4-Occasionally	5-Frequently	6-Always
1. Develop and mentor others through formal and informal approaches	☐	☐	☐	☐	☐	☐
2. Generate excitement and commitment for Centennial's vision and mandate within my department and with external stakeholders	☐	☐	☐	☐	☐	☐
3. Communicate changing stakeholders' needs to internal teams and adapt strategies accordingly	☐	☐	☐	☐	☐	☐
4. Actively seek out opportunities to partner with peers to champion initiatives internally	☐	☐	☐	☐	☐	☐
5. Motivate teams and individuals by communicating a clear sense of purpose	☐	☐	☐	☐	☐	☐
6. Seek out opportunities to demonstrate increased leadership in my present role	☐	☐	☐	☐	☐	☐

Plan for the Future
By taking a longer-term perspective, anticipates the implications of emerging academic and economic trends, and spots promising opportunities that align with the strategic priorities of the College

	1-Never	2-Very Rarely	3-Rarely	4-Occasionally	5-Frequently	6-Always
1. Model the College's values and help others understand their importance	☐	☐	☐	☐	☐	☐

2. Focus on supporting high quality teaching and learning	☐	☐	☐	☐	☐	☐
3. Identify areas of personal strength and capacity, as well as areas for development	☐	☐	☐	☐	☐	☐
4. Set development goals and work to achieve them	☐	☐	☐	☐	☐	☐
5. Look for opportunities for innovation across the College	☐	☐	☐	☐	☐	☐
6. Align development goals with the College's Vision (transforming lives and communities through learning) and Mission (educating students for career success)	☐	☐	☐	☐	☐	☐
7. Identify opportunities to support and mentor others	☐	☐	☐	☐	☐	☐
8. Seek support and mentorship from others	☐	☐	☐	☐	☐	☐
9. Translate vision and strategies into tangible actions and plans	☐	☐	☐	☐	☐	☐

Lead with Honesty, Integrity and Ethics
Exbibits uncompromising integrity and commitment to values, human resource principles and business conduct policies. Builds trust and instills self-confidence through mutually respectful, ongoing communication.

	1-Never	2-Very Rarely	3-Rarely	4-Occasionally	5-Frequently	6-Always
1. Demonstrate a strong work ethic and a high level of commitment to the College and its diverse student body	☐	☐	☐	☐	☐	☐
2. Give credit and acknowledge performance of colleagues and staff	☐	☐	☐	☐	☐	☐
3. Follow through on commitments	☐	☐	☐	☐	☐	☐
4. Provide necessary information and resources to internal teams to ensure commitments to stakeholder are met	☐	☐	☐	☐	☐	☐

	1-Never	2-Very Rarely	3-Rarely	4-Occasionally	5-Frequently	6-Always
5. Deliver timely and constructive feedback and encourages my managers to also do so	☐	☐	☐	☐	☐	☐
6. Accept team feedback and make focused decisions	☐	☐	☐	☐	☐	☐
7. Seek out and incorporate suggestions and ideas from others	☐	☐	☐	☐	☐	☐
8. Make decisions informed by professional guidelines and policies	☐	☐	☐	☐	☐	☐
9. Provide candid, but respectful, feedback to others	☐	☐	☐	☐	☐	☐

Model Leadership in a Diverse, Global Environment
The diversity that is at the core of Centennial's student population and in our workforce, demands that leaders understand the basis of inclusion and social justice. We are committed to leading the internationalization of the learning environment for all.

	1-Never	2-Very Rarely	3-Rarely	4-Occasionally	5-Frequently	6-Always
1. Challenge myself to seek out new learning and service opportunities	☐	☐	☐	☐	☐	☐
2. Actively seek out opportunities to partner with peers to champion initiatives internally	☐	☐	☐	☐	☐	☐
3. Link with external partners to build on each-others' innovative and entrepreneurial initiatives	☐	☐	☐	☐	☐	☐
4. Recognize and affirm multiple ways of knowing and being	☐	☐	☐	☐	☐	☐
5. Actively promote equity and inclusion	☐	☐	☐	☐	☐	☐
6. Create an environment open to diverse perspectives	☐	☐	☐	☐	☐	☐

Your Reflections

Upon completing this activity, reflect on your leadership competency and skills using the following questions as a guide:

1. What did you learn about yourself from this activity? What surprised you?

_____

_____

_____

2. What do you do well? (It is OK to congratulate yourself!)

_____

_____

_____

3. What change(s) would you like to consider right now? In the future?

_____

_____

_____

4. SoTL: How will this impact what you know, what you value, and how you will act (i.e., impact on your scholarly teaching and/or contributions to teaching and learning scholarship)?

_____

_____

_____

Interacting with Students

Each day you will interact with dozens of students outside of your teaching role. These numerous interactions may include informal break time conversations, academic advising during office hours or more formal appeal meetings. These are primarily private conversations with individual students and are rarely in the presence of other faculty. However, this means that you seldom receive any feedback on how you perform in these roles. Who better to provide valuable feedback in this area than a fellow faculty member?

Q

Activity 17: Call Another Friend

In this activity, you will invite another colleague to provide peer-to-peer feedback. Ideally, this process could be reciprocated with both participants providing feedback to each other. The goal is to receive feedback that can help you reflect on your interactions with your students outside of the classroom.

Identifying and asking a colleague to join you in this process is a key step. Consider the other person's experience, style of interacting with students and strengths. There is value in selecting someone who you perceive to have a similar style to you. However, do not ignore the potential value of selecting someone who you feel may have a different style. These individuals may be able to offer unique and thought-provoking insights that can influence your student interactions. It is important to also respect the privacy of the students and seek permission or ensure that identifying information is excluded from written work you may share.

Prior to approaching a fellow faculty member to join you in this activity, consider the various facets of your position. In terms of student interaction, which activities would you most value having another faculty sit in with you to observe and provide feedback? Here are some examples to consider:

- Course level academic advising
- Student appeal meetings
- Class break-time conversations
- Meeting to discuss a breach of academic integrity with a student.

You could also consider asking a fellow faculty member to provide feedback on your written communication to students or stakeholders. Examples might include:

- Email communications (e.g., in response to a student concern)
- Feedback on assignments
- Assignment descriptions
- Course handouts
- Article for publication
- Proposal for research or conference presentation
- Research or funding proposal
- Open Educational Resource (OER) you have created.

Upon reflection, complete the following action plan below, outlining the actions you will take:

My Action Plan			
I Would Like to Be Observed and Receive Feedback On:	**The Colleague I Will Ask Is:**	**Date/Time:**	**Outcomes and Lessons Learned:**

Your Reflections

After completing this activity, reflect on what it was like to receive feedback on your interactions with students and/or written communication using the following questions as a guide:

1. What did you learn about yourself from this activity? What surprised you?

_____

_____

_____

2. What do you do well? (It is OK to congratulate yourself!)

_____

_____

_____

3. What change(s) would you like to consider right now? In the future?

_____

_____

_____

4. SoTL: How will this impact what you know, what you value, and how you will act (i.e., impact on your scholarly teaching and/or contributions to teaching and learning scholarship)?

_____

_____

_____

Your Relationship with Your Supervisor

One of your most important relationships as a faculty member is the one that you have with your boss. Your Chairperson is the person who communicates with you how the strategic directions and college directives will shape the work of your School or division, and also helps guide you in your growth towards teaching excellence. Your Chairperson can offer you valuable coaching and mentorship when you are facing difficult situations or decisions, and is able to champion your ideas by mobilizing institutional supports or resources. Open and reciprocal communication and collaboration are essential to your success as a faculty member.

It is highly worthwhile to pay close attention to the feedback you receive from your Chairperson. Their ideas, suggestions, and recommendations can help you to align yourself and your work with the overall goals, directions, and values of your department. Every interaction with your Chairperson is a chance for you to learn and reflect.

Your Chairperson can give you feedback about your teaching practice through casual conversations, one-to-one meetings, reflective practice discussions, and through coaching or mentorship. When your relationship with your Chairperson is characterized by trust, reciprocity, collegiality, respect, and warmth, your mutual discussions will be enjoyable and satisfying. However, all great relationships require commitment, and your relationship with your boss is no exception. The following section will provide you with tools that can enhance your working relationship with your Chairperson. As you strive for excellence in your teaching practice, it is essential that you develop and maintain a good working relationship with your boss!

Activity 18: A Word with the Boss

This activity is to be completed in two steps. In the first part of this activity, you will reflect on how you feel about your relationship with your Chairperson. Answering the series of questions outlined below will offer you some 'diagnostics' about particular areas of focus. Step Two will ask you to put yourself in your Chairperson's shoes. You will consider how your Chairperson sees your work, attitude, approach and abilities. Taken together, the learning from both perspectives can offer you some powerful insights and a potential plan for action.

Step One: My Point of View

Take a few minutes and consider the following questions. Write the first ideas that come to mind. Be candid and don't overthink it!

1. To what extent do I feel at ease with my Chairperson during one-to-one meetings? What makes me comfortable or uncomfortable?

_____

_____

_____

2. How comfortable am I raising sensitive topics or offering honest opinions in group meetings when my Chairperson is present? What can sometimes hold me back from sharing?

_____

_____

_____

3. Am I able to effectively raise challenging topics or alternative perspectives with my Chairperson? What would make it easier for me to do so?

_____

_____

_____

4. How do I respond when my Chairperson gives me a directive that I do not necessarily agree with or am comfortable with?

_____

_____

_____

5. How well do I understand the expectations that my Chairperson has of me? What are the areas I am unclear or uncertain about?

_____

_____

_____

6. To what extent do I feel supported by my Chairperson? In what ways are they helpful and/or less helpful to me and my work?

_____

_____

_____

7. Does my Chairperson recognize my efforts and achievements? What kinds of recognition are most meaningful to me? How do I like to be acknowledged?

_____

_____

_____

8. Does my Chairperson support my work/life balance? What are my challenges in maintaining balance, and what supports do I need?

_____

_____

_____

9. Does my Chairperson ask my opinions and expertise about key decisions that will impact my work? How could I offer my ideas in ways that would have more impact and influence?

_____

_____

_____

Step Two: Another Point of View

All relationships are a two-way street. You may have one perspective and your Chairperson may have another. How do you think your Chairperson sees you? Consider the questions below, but this time from your Chairperson's perspective. The questions are rephrased slightly but they map on to similar concepts covered in the questions you asked yourself in Step One.

For this part of the activity, imagine that you are asking the following questions to your Chairperson and write down their responses. If there are any questions that are difficult to respond to from your Chairperson's point of view, make a note of it as this can be important information for reflection. Try not to overthink your responses – write down the first thoughts that come to your mind.

1. Do you feel at ease with me during our one-to-one meetings? How do I generally come across in our meetings?

    _____
    _____
    _____

2. Are you comfortable with how I raise sensitive topics or express my opinion in group meetings? What could I do to be more constructive?

    _____
    _____
    _____

3. Are you comfortable with how I raise issues or express my viewpoint in our one-to-one meetings? What could I do to be more effective or constructive?

    _____
    _____
    _____

4. How open am I to hearing your or others' thoughts and opinions when they differ from my own? What specific areas could I work on further?

    _____
    _____
    _____

5. Do I respond constructively when you give me a directive that I may not agree with? What would be more helpful and constructive in how I respond?

_____

_____

_____

6. To what extent do you think I understand your expectations of me? What are some areas that I am strong in meeting your expectations, and what are the areas of further development?

_____

_____

_____

7. To what extent do you feel that I support you in your role as Chairperson? How could I better support you as a faculty member?

_____

_____

_____

8. To what extent do I actively share with you my efforts and achievements? How could I better communicate these to you?

_____

_____

_____

9. How effectively do I manage my work/life balance? What suggestions do you have that would help me in managing balance more effectively?

_____

_____

_____

10. To what extent do I appropriately and effectively ask for your ideas and expertise on key decisions?

_____

_____

_____

11. To what extent do I appropriately and effectively offer my own ideas and expertise on key decisions?

_____

_____

_____

Review your responses to the questions in Step One and Step Two of this activity. What themes do you see? Were there any questions that were difficult to answer from your Chairperson's perspective? Are there areas where you need to do some additional 'soul-searching' or reflection?

Your willingness to courageously reflect on your working relationship with your boss can provide you with valuable food for thought. These insights can free up the space to see things differently and to engage with your Chairperson in new and productive ways. Not only will this strengthen your relationship with your Chairperson and support you in your teaching practice, this will also assist you in advancing your own career development and satisfaction over the longer term.

Based on your reflections and learning, choose a few of the above questions and ask for a coaching conversation with your Chairperson to focus on your relationship. How can you work together even more effectively? Use the following chart to plan the agenda for your meeting and jot down key takeaways following the meeting.

Date of Meeting:
Questions I will ask:
Outcomes and Implications for my Learning and Development:

Your Reflections

Upon completing this activity, reflect on what it was like to think about your working relationship with your Chairperson from different perspectives using the following questions as a guide:

1. What did you learn about yourself from this activity? What surprised you?

_____

_____

_____

2. What do you do well? (It is OK to congratulate yourself!)

_____

_____

_____

3. What change(s) would you like to consider right now? In the future?

_____

_____

_____

4. SoTL: How will this impact what you know, what you value, and how you will act (i.e., impact on your scholarly teaching and/or contributions to teaching and learning scholarship)?

_____

_____

_____

Classroom Management

At some level, every faculty member dreams of classes full of students who come to every class prepared to learn and are attentive, participatory, and engaged throughout the class. The reality is that students bring their differing histories, standpoints, abilities, personalities, past educational experiences, and personal challenges to each class and this sometimes presents challenges in facilitating positive, engaging and inclusive learning environments. Faculty have a responsibility to create a classroom environment that facilitates learning for all students and therefore we must be prepared to minimize, de-escalate, and respond to disruptive student behavior.

Centennial College has a *Disruptive Student Behaviour in the Classroom and other Learning Environments Policy* that provides guidance for faculty in how to respond to students' behavior, however invoking the policy is generally a last resort. Through preventative measures faculty can play a key role in setting a classroom climate that minimizes the opportunities for disruptions. Your response to minor disruptions can also de-escalate situations and avoid the necessity for formal, disciplinary interventions.

Activity 19: Managing Your Classroom

In this activity, you will consider strategies that both help to prevent and minimize disruptive student behaviour in the classroom. Take a moment and identify which strategies you use.

Do you...?	Response		Example/Comments
Establish a respectful relationship with students?	☐	Yes	
	☐	No	
Consistently use a respectful tone when speaking to students?	☐	Yes	
	☐	No	
Establish clear classroom norms to guide procedures such as asking questions or participating in discussions?	☐	Yes	
	☐	No	
Intentionally create an inclusive, safe, respectful environment?	☐	Yes	
	☐	No	
Use inclusive language and ensure that others do as well?	☐	Yes	
	☐	No	
Regularly utilize strategies for collaboration?	☐	Yes	
	☐	No	

Reinforce desired student behaviours (e.g. teamwork, engagement, effort)?	☐ Yes ☐ No	
Respond to disruptive behavior using non-confrontational techniques (e.g., movement throughout class, change of teaching strategy, pause, questioning)?	☐ Yes ☐ No	
Defuse tough situations and potential conflicts?	☐ Yes ☐ No	
Avoid power struggles?	☐ Yes ☐ No	
Maintain self-control?	☐ Yes ☐ No	
Anticipate and plan for potential problems?	☐ Yes ☐ No	
Consider how you are contributing (i.e., pace of class, engagement of students, active learning)?	☐ Yes ☐ No	

What other activities that are you doing that are not listed above, yet you feel contribute to minimizing disruptive student behavior?

_____
_____
_____
_____
_____
_____

Review your answers to the above checklist and congratulate yourself on those that you are already implementing. These are the actions that you can take to ensure your students feel valued and respected during their time at college. Also pause to consider those points for which you replied 'no', or those for which you hesitated before answering. Is there a practice you would like to try in your next class? Consider what you would like to change and record it in the table below:

Date of Implementation:
Strategies I will try:
Outcomes and implications for my learning and development:

Your Reflections

Upon completing this activity, reflect on what it was like to explore your classroom management skills using the following questions as a guide:

1. What did you learn about yourself from this activity? What surprised you?

_____
_____
_____

2. What do you do well? (It is OK to congratulate yourself!)

_____
_____
_____

3. What change(s) would you like to consider right now? In the future?

_____
_____
_____

4. SoTL: How will this impact what you know, what you value, and how you will act (i.e., impact on your scholarly teaching and/or contributions to teaching and learning scholarship)?

_____

_____

_____

Inclusive Pedagogy

According to the Center for New Designs in Teaching and Scholarship at Georgetown University, inclusive pedagogy can be defined as follows:

> *"Inclusive pedagogy means taking a student-centered approach to teaching that pays attention to the varied background, learning styles, and abilities of all the learners in front of you. It is a method of teaching in which instructors and students work together to create a supportive and open environment that fosters social justice and allows each individual to be fully present and feel equally valued.*
>
> *Inclusive pedagogy at its core is learner-centered and equity-focused, creating an overarching learning environment in which students feel equally invited and included. Drawing from a large body of research—much of it foundational scholarship on teaching and learning—it is clear that learning outcomes are improved for everyone when teachers attend to student differences and take deliberate steps to ensure that all students, across differences in academic and social background as well as physical and cognitive abilities, feel welcomed, valued, challenged, and supported in their academic work."* (Center for New Designs in Teaching and Scholarship, n.d.).

Previously you may have reflected on your ability to foster an inclusive classroom in *Activity 10: Is Your Classroom Welcoming and Safe?* The activities found in this section ask you to step back from your classroom to explore inclusivity within your curriculum and teaching practice. A safe and supportive learning environment can be impacted by your teaching style, the content you share, and how you communicate. The activities[3] in this section require you to ask yourself some difficult questions about every aspect of your teaching.

---

[3] We would like to acknowledge Yasmin Razack and Helen Anderson for contributing these activities.

Q

Activity 20: Diversity in Curriculum and Teaching Practice

Integrating elements of diversity that foster inclusive pedagogy can work to increase engagement and student success. The chart below provides an opportunity for you to identify areas of strength in your teaching practice as well as areas for growth. Check the elements of diversity you have integrated in you teaching practice and the type of approach you have used (see list of approaches following the chart).

Elements of Diversity	Integrated?	Approach Used
Indigenous Peoples (e.g., First Nations, Inuit, Métis, global Indigenous communities, etc.)		
Race and Ethnicity (e.g., people of colour/racialized people, cultural minorities, mixed race people, etc.)		
Socioeconomic/Employment Status (e.g., low income, unemployed, precariously employed, etc.)		
Sex/Gender (e.g., male, female, women, men, trans, two-spirit, intersex, etc.)		
Differing Abilities (e.g., physical, D/deaf, deafened or hard of hearing, blind or low vision, intellectual/developmental, learning, mental illness, addictions/substance use, etc.)		
Language (e.g., learners whose first language is not English, literacy as it affects communication, etc.)		
Religious/Faith/Spiritual Communities		
Sexual Orientation (e.g., lesbian, gay, bisexual, etc.)		
Geographical Area (e.g., rural/remote or inner-urban populations, geographic or social isolation, under-serviced areas, etc.)		
International Perspectives (e.g., outside of Euro-North American or colonial frameworks)		
Age (e.g., children, youth, mature students, seniors, etc.)		

Citizenship Status (e.g., refugees, immigrants, undocumented people, temporary foreign workers, etc.)		
People Living in Institutions (e.g., hospital settings, group homes, detention centres, prisons, long-term care facilities, etc.)		
Housing Status (e.g., under-housed, street involved, without a fixed address, couch surfing, community-supported housing, etc.)		
Other (please describe):		

Type of approach used (Adapted from Kea & Trent, 2013):
- **CA**: Contributions Approach (i.e., celebrates holidays, heroes, and discrete cultural events).
- **AA**: Additive Approach (i.e., adds content, concepts, themes and perspectives to the curriculum without changing its basic structure).
- **TA**: Transformative Approach (i.e., requires a change in the structure of the curriculum to enable students to view concepts, issues, events and themes from the perspective of diverse groups).
- **SA**: Social Action Approach (i.e., encourages students to make decisions on important social issues and take actions to solve them).

Activity 21: Assessing Inclusive Pedagogy
In this activity, you will have an opportunity to reflect on your success in supporting inclusive pedagogy. The following chart includes questions for consideration. Upon reflection, identify two things you are currently doing that are reflective of the questions asked and identify two new things you will try to address any gaps or shortcomings.

Self-Reflection	
How does my gender, race, abilities, socioeconomic status, sexual orientation, faith, etc. influence the way I interact with students and colleagues? How do my own beliefs, values and experiences shape my interactions with students and colleagues?	Two Things I Have Done: Two Things I Will Try:
Representation in the College Environment	
How have I included diverse groups and their experiences in my course materials, readings, assignments, etc.? How do I challenge stereotypes and assumptions with my students and colleagues?	Two Things I Have Done: Two Things I Will Try:
Addressing Power and Privilege	
How do I identify, address, and eliminate the biases, barriers, and power dynamics that prevent students from participating fully in learning? How do I use my power and	Two Things I Have Done:

privilege as a faculty member to advocate for greater equity? How do I encourage students to question their own power and privilege as college students?	Two Things I Will Try:
Taking Action	
How do I ensure students are comfortable to speak out if they have a concern related to inclusivity? Do students feel safe to speak out in my classroom? How do I ensure students feel respected and valued in my classroom?	Two Things I Have Done: Two Things I Will Try:
Access to Learning	
How do I ensure that my teaching style, course materials, and classroom practices are accessible for everyone (e.g., literacy levels, images reflective of diverse groups, extra support as required)? Do my students recognize who has access (i.e., socially, physically, etc.) to higher education and who does not? Do I?	Two Things I Have Done: Two Things I Will Try:

Accountability to Diversity	
To what extent do I acknowledge my own privilege and power as a faculty member? How do I make my students and classroom practices accountable (i.e., promoting diversity, addressing stereotypes, etc. in materials and within the classroom environment)? How do I address problematic student behavior, comments, etc., within and outside of my class (e.g., intentional and unintentional racism)? Are there places I can turn for support and resources to ensure I'm supporting diversity?	Two Things I Have Done: Two Things I Will Try:

Participation and Engagement	
How do I identify and address barriers to my student's ability to participate and engage with my course material? And with each other? How do I interact with students from groups that experience inequity (e.g., am I fair, lenient, harsh)?	Two Things I Have Done: Two Things I Will Try:

How do I make sure my students interact in respectful ways?	
Overlapping and Intersecting Social Identities	
How do I highlight the ways in which my student's different identities may intersect and impact one another (e.g., gender, race, class, age, religion, etc.)? How do the different parts of my own identity impact one other?	Two Things I Have Done:
	Two Things I Will Try:

Your Reflections

Upon completing the activities above, reflect on your experience exploring inclusive pedagogy using the following questions as a guide:

1. What did you learn about yourself from this activity? What surprised you?

_____

_____

_____

2. What do you do well? (It is OK to congratulate yourself!)

_____

_____

_____

3. What change(s) would you like to consider right now? In the future?

_____

_____

_____

4. SoTL: How will this impact what you know, what you value, and how you will act (i.e., impact on your scholarly teaching and/or contributions to teaching and learning scholarship)?

_____

_____

_____

Universal Design for Learning – How Accessible is Your Course?

Most of us are comfortable with the term 'accommodation' and how it applies to our work as faculty. We understand that our role is to provide individuals with adaptions to our teaching and evaluation strategies, allowing them equitable access to student opportunities. When providing accommodation with a student, this represents an individualized approach. We are presented with a specific situation and in response, provide an individualized solution. This differs from the principles of Universal Design for Learning (UDL).

An approach based on the principles of Universal Design is proactive and strives to plan for classroom (online and face-to-face) and learning experiences that are usable by all. Ryerson University, defines UDL as:

> *"The design of instructional materials and activities that allow learning goals to be achieved by individuals with wide differences in their abilities to see, hear, speak, move, read, write, understand English, attend, organize, engage, and remember. The Essential qualities of UDL Include valuing each learner's unique perspectives and accommodating individual differences in learners' backgrounds, interests, abilities, and experiences. The Cardinal rule of UDL Is that there is no single method for representing information that will provide equal access for all students; no single method of expression that will provide equal opportunity for all students; no single way to ensure that all students are engaged in learning because any method that works for some students may present barriers to learning for others. Accordingly, Universal Instructional Design Emphasize flexibility in curriculum and instruction."* (Ryerson University, 2012).

The application of UDL principles is holistic and may encompass the entire course structure, including the design of the course materials, offering of student supports, teaching, and assessment methodology.

Sue Wells, Lisa McCaie, Megan Barker & Marilyn Herie

Activity 22: Do You Integrate UDL in Your Course Design?

In this activity[4] the focus will be on your delivery of one of your courses and the evaluation strategies within that course. You will be asked to reflect on best practices in UDL and your success at embedding these principles in a course that you teach. This activity can be completed individually or with a faculty member who teaches different sections of the same course. Select a course and consider the following questions:

When delivering a course do you…

Topic	Rating (5 = consistently, 1=seldom)				
Identify course objectives and learning outcomes?	5	4	3	2	1
Deliver course expectations explicitly and in multiple formats (e.g., verbally, on the course outline, on the course web page)?	5	4	3	2	1
Use multiple means of presenting material in class, including, where appropriate, lecturing, activities (e.g., demonstrations, laboratories, group projects, case studies), video, technology, etc.?	5	4	3	2	1
Present single concepts in more than one way (e.g. a demonstration followed by a lecture explaining relevant concepts)	5	4	3	2	1
Use slides that are easy to read (i.e., large font, not too text-heavy) if using presentation materials?	5	4	3	2	1
Encourage natural supports within the classroom setting (e.g., peer-to-peer mentoring, use of office hours, teaching assistants, study groups, opportunities for questions, etc.)?	5	4	3	2	1
Encourage faculty-student engagement (e.g., use of office hours, email, web postings, discussion boards, etc.)?	5	4	3	2	1

---

[4] This activity has been adapted with permission from Ryerson University's *Universal Design for Learning* (2012) which can be retrieved from: http://www.ryerson.ca/content/dam/lt/resources/instructionaldesign/UDLRecommendations.pdf

Use technology to enhance learning (e.g., clickers, Google drive, web 2.0, etc.)?	5 4 3 2 1
Post notes for difficult concepts or provide a simplified version of the slides used in class?	5 4 3 2 1
Use moderate language when lecturing, replacing terms such as "this or that" with specific descriptions?	5 4 3 2 1
Encourage student participation in multiple ways (e.g., questions, small groups, pairing students, discussions, etc.)?	5 4 3 2 1
Create guided notes (i.e., notes where some material is left off) that students can use during lecture?	5 4 3 2 1
Update course material annually keeping the course relevant and current?	5 4 3 2 1
Repeat important concepts and provide additional examples of these concepts?	5 4 3 2 1
Connect important course concepts to real life through the use of news stories, personal stories, research stories, and case studies?	5 4 3 2 1
Assist students, especially semester one students, in learning study techniques, improving writing and numeracy?	5 4 3 2 1
Provide materials to students before class so that they may print or use the materials as a guide during lectures?	5 4 3 2 1
Review the previous classes' content at the beginning of class and allow students to ask questions? Do you then summarize important points at the end of each class?	5 4 3 2 1
Give students a short break part way through class?	5 4 3 2 1
Allow students to record lectures or use note takers?	5 4 3 2 1
Repeat students' questions before responding?	5 4 3 2 1
Ensure that all students can see and hear you when lecturing, as well as see the PowerPoint or board?	5 4 3 2 1
Use captioned videos?	5 4 3 2 1

Allow students the option to ask questions without raising their hand?	5	4	3	2	1
Provide verbal explanations for PowerPoint slides, material on the board, and any graphs or charts used in class?	5	4	3	2	1
Provide printed materials in black and white?	5	4	3	2	1
Use a textbook that is available electronically as well as in print editions (i.e., offering it in larger print)?	5	4	3	2	1
Identify any student in need of accommodations in laboratories (if relevant) and ensure that all chemicals and equipment are clearly labeled?	5	4	3	2	1

When designing assessments for a course do you…

Topic	Rating (5 = consistently, 1=seldom)				
Create learning assessments that assess course goals and that are designed in a backwards manner (i.e., backward design begins by developing course objectives and then outlining appropriate means of assessing whether these objectives have been met by students in a way that reflects the course goals)?	5	4	3	2	1
Create assessments that are flexible and use a combination of modes of expression (e.g., writing, speaking, drawing, creating, presenting) to demonstrate the understanding of course content?	5	4	3	2	1
Offer multiple methods of assessment for each assignment?	5	4	3	2	1
Provide flexible deadlines and allow for negotiation, avoiding deadlines that are too harsh?	5	4	3	2	1
Provide opportunities for feedback throughout the process of completing a larger assignment?	5	4	3	2	1

How can you challenge yourself to apply the principles of UDL? Once you have completed the surveys, review the results and determine actions that you would like to implement in the next semester, allowing all of your students to reach their learning potential.

My Action Plan			
I Would Like to Make the Following Changes to Implement UDL Principles:	**Resources I will Review to do This Are:**	**Date/Time:**	**Outcomes and Lessons Learned:**

Your Reflections

Take a moment to think about your experience putting the survey together and receiving feedback from your students. You can use the following questions as a guide:

1. What did you learn about yourself from this activity? What surprised you?

_____
_____
_____

2. What do you do well? (It is OK to congratulate yourself!)

_____
_____
_____

3. What change(s) would you like to consider right now? In the future?

_____

_____

_____

4. SoTL: How will this impact what you know, what you value, and how you will act (i.e., impact on your scholarly teaching and/or contributions to teaching and learning scholarship)?

_____

_____

_____

Policies to Support Inclusivity at the College: An Opportunity for Reflection

To operationalize a commitment to diversity, Centennial College has implemented policies and practices to address issues of inclusion among faculty, staff, and learners. As faculty, you are accountable to uphold, administer, and safeguard the principles outlined in these guiding documents to support an accessible and inclusive learning environment. Examples of such policies and practices include the following:

Policies
- Student Accommodation Policy – Facilitating Learning and Success
- Religious Accommodation Procedures
- Family Accommodation Procedures
- Accommodation Procedures for Students with Disabilities
- Student Mental Health Crisis Intervention Protocol

Reflect on the following key strategies to ensure the protection and promotion of inclusivity policies at the College. Check off the strategies you currently practice and set goals for items you may have missed and would like to implement in the future:

- ☐ I have read the College's policies and guidelines as they relate to issues of inclusion.
- ☐ I understand the principles outlined in these policies.
- ☐ If I do not understand what I have read in these policies, I have asked my Department Chair for clarification.
- ☐ I know that it is my responsibility to implement and safeguard the principles outlined in these policies.
- ☐ I actively implement the guiding principles in the College's policies as they relate to issues of inclusion.
- ☐ When faced with a potential issue that may go against the guiding principles outlined in these policies, I refer to the relevant document to determine what to do next.
- ☐ If my students are experiencing an issue as it relates to inclusion, I feel comfortable sharing with them the relevant policy to support them in navigating their next steps.
- ☐ I know where to direct my students and/or support them if they require accommodation.

Moving forward, I will implement the following strategies to ensure my active protection and promotion of inclusivity policies at the College:

_____

_____

_____

_____

Protecting Privacy

As a faculty member, you are governed by the Freedom of Information and Privacy Act (FIPA) and therefore have a professional responsibility to safeguard the privacy of your students. This responsibility extends to all records including drafts, post-it notes, notations in electronic systems, emails, mobile device files, agendas, notes in notebooks, and verbal disclosure of information. Faculty are typically aware and vigilant when formal requests for student information or whereabouts are received, referring these requests to the Freedom of Information Officer and following other appropriate procedures. However, it is also important to remember that private student information should always be safeguarded by faculty.

Activity 23: How Careful Are You?

In this activity[5] you will reflect on best practices for protecting the privacy of students and compare them to your own practices, identifying where you could improve your procedures. During this process, you will consider general privacy practices and those that apply specifically to instructional technology and your faculty role. Additionally, you will also consider the unique privacy concerns when you have encounters with your student's family members. Reflect on the following list of best privacy practices and rate yourself on the scale provided (1=never and 5=always).

Privacy Best Practices: General Considerations					
Do you...	1-Never	2- Rarely	3-Occasionally	4-Frequently	5-Always
1. Leave your desk clean ensuring all documents containing personal information are kept in a locked drawer?	☐	☐	☐	☐	☐
2. Ensure your computer is locked (password-protected) when you leave your desk?	☐	☐	☐	☐	☐
3. Securely destroy information when you no longer need it?	☐	☐	☐	☐	☐
4. Only review private information that is necessary for your role?	☐	☐	☐	☐	☐

---

[5] We would like to acknowledge Thomas Nault for contributing this activity.

	1-Never	2- Rarely	3-Occasionally	4-Frequently	5-Always
5. Refrain from taking confidential information off campus?	☐	☐	☐	☐	☐
6. Request permission from your manager to take confidential items off campus?	☐	☐	☐	☐	☐
7. Make copies instead of taking home originals, if taking confidential items offsite?	☐	☐	☐	☐	☐
8. Keep the files secure at all times (i.e., never left in an unattended car), if taking confidential items offsite?	☐	☐	☐	☐	☐
9. Write in a professional manner?	☐	☐	☐	☐	☐
10. Eliminate unnecessary copies, drafts and previous versions?	☐	☐	☐	☐	☐
11. Use gender neutral language as appropriate or use language the student is comfortable with (i.e., confirm student's pronouns)?	☐	☐	☐	☐	☐
Privacy Best Practices: IT Considerations					
1. Refrain from saving confidential information to a USB?	☐	☐	☐	☐	☐
2. Encrypt all devices?	☐	☐	☐	☐	☐
3. Use caution when using an external service to transmit information?	☐	☐	☐	☐	☐
Privacy Best Practices: Working with Students					
1. Try to verify identity of the student (i.e., using a Centennial email address) when communicating with students?	☐	☐	☐	☐	☐
2. Seek student permission if you wish to video or audio record or photograph the students in class (i.e., giving presentations)?	☐	☐	☐	☐	☐
3. Seek student permission to share their work in class unless it is certain it can be anonymized so other students cannot identify the author?	☐	☐	☐	☐	☐
4. Only collect information in class needed for the administration of the class and only use the information collected for the reason it was collected?	☐	☐	☐	☐	☐
5. Refrain from passing attendance sheets where students can see the information of other students?	☐	☐	☐	☐	☐
6. Refrain from requiring students to put their full student numbers on group assignments?	☐	☐	☐	☐	☐
7. Take care to protect personal information when students submit for classroom accommodations?	☐	☐	☐	☐	☐

	1-Never	2- Rarely	3-Occasionally	4-Frequently	5-Always
8. Ensure that drop off locations for assignments are secure and cannot easily be broken into?	☐	☐	☐	☐	☐
9. Return student work directly to the student?	☐	☐	☐	☐	☐
10. Properly dispose of student work that is not claimed by the student?	☐	☐	☐	☐	☐
11. Place grade information and written comments on an inside page of assignment or tests?	☐	☐	☐	☐	☐
12. Refrain from publicly posting grade lists?	☐	☐	☐	☐	☐
13. Use only a portion of the student number, and ensure the list is not in alphabetical order, if grades are publicly posted?	☐	☐	☐	☐	☐
Privacy Best Practices: Working with Students and Their Families					
1. Receive consent from student (written is preferred) without the family member present before discussing an issue with a family member?	☐	☐	☐	☐	☐
2. Make a note of the circumstances if only verbal consent is received and who was present in the discussion?	☐	☐	☐	☐	☐
3. Limit duration of consent to as short of a window as possible (i.e., this meeting only)?	☐	☐	☐	☐	☐
Privacy Best Practices: Loss of Confidential Information					
1. Inform your manager right away in the event that confidential student information is lost or compromised?	☐	☐	☐	☐	☐

Your Reflections

Upon completing this activity, reflect on your ability to support privacy best practices by using the following questions as a guide:

1. What did you learn about yourself from this activity? What surprised you?

_____
_____
_____

2. What do you do well? (It is OK to congratulate yourself!)

_____

_____

_____

3. What change(s) would you like to consider right now? In the future?

_____

_____

_____

4. SoTL: How will this impact what you know, what you value, and how you will act (i.e., impact on your scholarly teaching and/or contributions to teaching and learning scholarship)?

_____

_____

_____

Interested in further reflection regarding privacy issues?
You may wish to extend reflection regarding privacy issues through discussion with colleagues. Consider adding one of the following case studies to the agenda at your next faculty meeting or discuss over a coffee with a few colleagues. As you read through the cases consider the following questions. What are the key issues in these cases? How would you mitigate these issues?

Case Study #1: You receive a call from an upset parent who wants to know what their child's (your student's) marks are. They insist they have the right to know since they paid tuition for their child's (your student's) education. How would you handle the situation? How would you handle the situation if the parent arrived in your office with their child (your student)?

Case Study #2: You have been asked by your Chairperson to design a form to collect student preferences for extra support sessions. They have asked you to collect the following student information: name, student number, gender, address, and birthdate. How should you proceed?

Part Four: Taking Action

"The future depends on what you do today."

- Gandhi

In this section, you will have an opportunity to think about where you were when you started in your reflective practice journey, and where you are now. This section will prepare you to take the next steps through the following activities:
- Preparing for Reflective Practice Meetings
- Stretch Yourself!

How will you begin to make changes based on what you've learned?

Pulling It All Together

Reflective practice is valuable in confirming what you are doing well. That validation can affirm the results of your efforts, your skills, and your intentions. Although positive feedback feels great and will motivate you to keep moving forward, reflective practice can also help you to identify areas for change or improvement. Receiving feedback that requires you to make a change can sometimes be difficult to hear or absorb. It can also be challenging to make sense of where you should go next. You're already working so hard, what more can you do?

Behaviour change is most effective when clear and measurable goals have been identified. Professional development activities such as workshops, conferences, and trainings can play a vital role in enhancing your teaching practice. Yet, despite good intentions to implement new knowledge and skills post-training, translating lessons learned into day-to-day practice is not always easy or feasible. To make sustainable changes to your teaching practice through reflective practice, you might need to take a 'non-traditional' approach.

Changing your teaching practice is a process, not an event. Meaningful change requires persistent attention to how you engage with your work, colleagues, and students. Although it is not always intentional, each interaction and every teaching moment conveys to others who you are and what you stand for as a faculty member.

The rich data that you have collected through the activities in *Part Two* and *Part Three* of this manual and your reflections on this data will have revealed to you the inconsistencies or gaps about who you want to be, what you value, and how you come across to others. The areas of disconnect between your actions and your aspirational vision of yourself as a faculty member offer you a personalized roadmap for change.

As a way to get yourself started, review the data you have collected throughout the activities in this manual and identify three areas that you would like to change within the next three months:

1. _____
2. _____
3. _____

Taking Reflection to Action

Identifying your focus for change is the first step in moving from reflecting on your practice to changing it. However, like a New Year's resolution that is often forgotten by February, you will have little success in changing your practice without an action plan. It is often easy to skip this step particularly when your desire for change feels like it will be enough to propel you into sustainable action. Instead, pause for a moment and consider those times when you wanted to make a change in your life like quitting smoking, losing weight, eating healthy, or balancing your work/life priorities. Think about what made you successful in changing this behaviour. Admit it, you probably had a plan! You may have put your goals in writing, kept track of progress, and set benchmarks for yourself. To put your reflections into tangible actions, here are a few tips to get you started:

- Use the **SMART** goal approach to set goals for yourself that are **S**pecific, **M**easurable, **A**ttainable, **R**elevant and **T**ime-Based. It is an effective, yet simple framework that can guide your actions towards change and measure your success.
- Identify the resources that can support your action plan. Don't forget about your colleagues – they can provide a wealth of knowledge!
- Remember to plan how you will measure your success. What results will you consider a success? Knowing this will help you to celebrate when you get there.

Activity 24: Preparing for Reflective Practice Meetings
Your Chairperson should meet with you at least once a year as an opportunity for you to reflect on the big picture. Unlike ongoing department or faculty meetings where the focus is often operational and

collective, annual meetings with your Chairperson can provide a valuable opportunity for you to focus on your teaching and your role as a faculty member. This is the time for you to take all that work that you do in the classroom (in-person and online), your office, the college hallways, and beyond, and celebrate it! Your manager won't know about the full scope of your work if you don't let them know about it. This is your opportunity to share and reflect.

In preparation for this meeting, consider the following topics for discussion by formulating a response:

Topic for Discussion	Prepared Response
What progress have you made on any goals that you set the previous year?	
What data have you collected from students, peers, and/or through self-reflection? Which data collection tools from this resource have you utilized? What did you learn from them?	
What new teaching practice or evaluation strategy did you try in the past academic year? How did it go?	
What new teaching practice or evaluation strategy are you planning on trying this academic year?	
What was your best 'teaching moment'?	
What do you consider to be your biggest strength as a teacher?	
Are there any obstacles that are preventing you from being the best teacher that you can be?	

What are they? How can your Chairperson help to mitigate them?	
What was your most remarkable achievement this past year? In what ways can your Chairperson support you in sharing this within your department or the College?	
What are your goals for next year? How can your Chairperson help to support them?	
How do you evaluate your success as a teacher? How can your Chairperson support your continued growth as a teacher?	
How are you using technology to enhance the learning experience for your students?	
Have you taught a hybrid or online course? If so, how have you evaluated its success?	
What strategies have you implemented to support student retention within the courses that you teach?	
What steps have you taken to create an inclusive classroom environment?	

Activity 25: Stretch Yourself!

Reflective practice meetings provide you with the opportunity to put voice and action to your dreams for growth and development. There is shift in higher education away from traditional views of research and publication to recognize and embrace multiple forms of scholarship. Remember Boyer's Model of Teaching and Scholarship from the *Introduction* section of this manual? Many colleges have integrated this model and its broader definition of scholarship to support and measure the scholarly outputs of faculty members.

Taking into consideration Boyer's Model, think about some additional scholarly activities that you could be doing as part of your personal and professional development. Fill out the following chart below and take it with you to your next reflective practice meeting. Dare to dream – and work with your Chairperson to put that dream into action!

Boyer's Model of Scholarship			
Type of Scholarship	**Purpose**	**Example Measures of Performance**	**What I Will Do?**
Discovery	Build new knowledge through traditional research	• Publishing in peer-reviewed forums • Producing and/or performing creative work within established field • Creating infrastructure for future research	
Integration	Interpret the use of knowledge across disciplines (and professions)	• Preparing a comprehensive literature review • Writing a textbook for use in multiple disciplines • Collaborating with colleagues to design and deliver a course	

Application	Aid society and professions in addressing problems	• Serving industry or government in a consultative or advisory role • Assuming leadership roles in professional organizations • Advising student leaders to foster their professional growth	
Teaching	Study teaching models to achieve optimal learning	• Advanced learning theory through classroom research • Developing and testing instructional materials • Mentoring/coaching students • Designing and implementing assessment systems • Developing and sharing Open Educational Resources (OERs) for others to use or adapt	

Conclusion

As a faculty member, you teach, motivate, inspire, and support students as they acquire the knowledge and skills to become successful professionals. Perhaps the most important role in the College, the work you do is critical to the success of students. The values you bring to this work affects how you teach and interact with students, colleagues, and your manager. Your reflection on this provides you with boundless opportunities to grow, learn, and improve.

This manual has offered you a roadmap for your reflective journey. You have identified your values and connected them to your teaching practice. You have reflected on how you have implemented your values into action. Along the way, you have read personal stories, lessons learned, and inspirations from your colleagues as they travelled through their own reflective practice journeys.

As we are also on our own reflective practice journeys, we welcome hearing your ideas of how we can expand and improve this guide for faculty members. An evaluation of this manual has been included for you to share with us your thoughts – we welcome your feedback!

This manual is just scratching the surface of the learnings that can occur during reflective practice. Your personal journey will add rich and valuable learnings beyond what has been shared here. We hope this guide has offered a useful point of departure for your ongoing journey of discovery, growth, and transformation. We wish you all the best as you continue to go forward, navigating the dynamic and exciting terrain of reflective practice.

About the Authors

Sue Wells MA ECE RT

I have been an academic leader for almost 20 years. In this role, I have the unique privilege of engaging in reflective practice discussions with all the faculty within the department. These are, by far, my favorite meetings of the year. It is through this experience that I get to learn about the innovation, passion and scholarship that our faculty bring to their profession and the depth of their reflections on the teaching and learning process. I am inspired by what faculty learn through reflective practice and am sharing the tools and ideas in this manual in the hope that others will become inspired as well.

Lisa McCaie BEd ECE RT

My path to becoming a full-time professor teaching Early Childhood Education at Centennial College, began when I become a graduate of the program. As a faculty member, Early Childhood Educator, Resource Educator, and alumni of Centennial, I've seen my reflective practice journey grow and develop throughout the years as I've engaged with these various roles. An important driver of my reflective practice is my passion towards children, their families, and for the field of Early Childhood Education. As a faculty member, I try to share and instill these same values with my students. I believe that the best learning happens when students are interested, engaged, challenged and supported. I hope this manual and the testimonials provided will be a source of inspiration as faculty enhance their own reflective practice journeys.

Megan Barker MA

As an Education Specialist within adult education, I have been developing, designing and delivering curriculum with healthcare providers for the past seven years. Reflective practice is the crux of the healthcare provider role - it can enhance professional skills, facilitate interprofessional communication, and improve patient outcomes. I am also on my own reflective practice journey as I complete my PhD in Public Health. As a critical qualitative researcher, I'm consistently called upon to reflect on my own assumptions, values, and biases as they relate to my research. It's been a journey of self-discovery and hopefully the tools provided in this manual will help others to chart their own pathways of reflective practice.

Marilyn Herie PhD RSW

From clinician-educator to postsecondary leadership, I have always been interested in reflective practice and the value it can bring to diverse contexts and roles. As an educator for over 20 years, I am truly amazed by the power of critical reflection to elicit new ways of thinking, knowing, and doing. By learning the limits of my knowledge and expertise through reflective practice, I have felt truly humbled but also inspired to maximize opportunities for personal growth and development. As an educator, it can sometimes feel difficult to be responsive to a diversity of student complexities, issues, and needs. However, reflecting on our practice in the moment can lead to actions that foster experiential, inclusive, and student-centred learning environments. The tools and ideas in this manual are meant to help faculty identify what they're doing well and where improvements can be made. I hope that these tools will have real impact in supporting reflective practice among faculty and enable transformative learning among students.

Resources for Further Learning

Books

Reflective Practice in Education Made Real: Reflection, Feedback, and Teaching

Robyn Brandenburg (2017)

Written for educators, this book includes successful reflective practice and feedback strategies from the teacher perspective, tools to integrate and adapt into teaching practice, examples of activities, and creative ways to introduce reflective practice in the classroom.

Reflective Practice for Educators: Professional Development to Improve Student Learning

Karen F. Osterman and Robert B. Kottkamp (2015)

An educator's guide to reflective practice, this book explores how reflective practice can lead to meaningful change in schools and improve student outcomes. It offers a critical perspective for change management and includes ideas and practical strategies for problem-solving, quality improvement, and implementation.

Reflective Practice: Writing and Professional Development

Gillie Bolton (2014)

This guide provides educators with strategies to engage in reflective practice through activities and exercises linked to pedagogical theories and values.

Reflective Practice and Professional Development

Peter Tarrant (2013)

This book includes ways to engage and enhance reflective practice, case studies, and useful resources to guide professional development. It also provides educators with the opportunity to develop their own reflective practice framework.

Teaching and Learning through Reflective Practice: A Practical Guide for Positive Action

Tony Ghaye (2011)

A practical guide for educators to learn through reflection exploring four fundamental questions – what is working well? What needs changing? What are we learning? Where do we go from here?

Websites

Centre for Organizational Learning and Teaching (COLT) at Centennial College

Includes professional development, eLearning, instruction, and technology resources to support faculty in developing and delivering curriculum within the college context.

centennialcollege.ca/COLT-CAQ

Higher Education Quality Council of Ontario

Explores key issues in higher education through evidence-based research in post-secondary education. Includes resources, a blog, and information regarding upcoming events.

http://www.heqco.ca/en-ca/

Reflective Practice: International and Multidisciplinary Perspectives

This journal is published four times per year and focuses exclusively on reflective practice, implications for teaching, learning, the workplace, and helping professionals.

http://www.tandfonline.com/loi/crep20

Teaching, Learning, and Everything Else: Conversations about Teaching in Higher Education

This podcast includes series of conversations with teachers in higher education reflecting on teaching issues. Online references are provided in each episode.

https://cat.xula.edu/food/topic/podcast/

Educause

A nonprofit association supporting educators to advance the use of technology in higher education. Includes links to resources, networking opportunities, and career development supports.

https://www.educause.edu/

The Professional and Organizational Development (Pod) Network

Advances research and practice of educational development in higher education. Includes publications, an interactive wiki, and forums to support faculty development.

http://podnetwork.org/

Educateria

Dr. Marilyn Herie PhD, RSW, Vice President Academic and Chief Learning Officer at Centennial College provides tips and reflections for educators and presenters.

https://educateria.com/

Evaluation: We want your feedback!
Faculty Leadership: A Reflective Practice Guide for Community College Faculty

We would like to continue to enhance this manual so your candid feedback is critical. Please take a moment to complete and return this brief evaluation form. Your evaluation will help us track the usefulness of the manual.

Demographic Questions

Please identify the school/area in which you work:

☐ The Business School

☐ School of Advancement

☐ School of Transportation

☐ School of Community and Health Studies

☐ School of Media, Communications, Art and Design

☐ School of Engineering Technology and Applied Sciences

☐ School of Hospitality, Tourism and Culinary Arts

☐ Libraries and Learning Centres

☐ Other (please specify):
_____

How are you employed by Centennial College?:

☐ Full-time

☐ Part-time

☐ Partial Load

☐ Sessional

☐ Other (please specify):
_____

Evaluation

Overall Satisfaction

Please rate the following as it relates to your overall satisfaction of this manual.

(Indicate your response by checking your answer)

	Strongly Disagree	Disagree	Neutral	Agree	Strongly Agree
1. Manual objectives were met through the content provided					
2. The manual was well-organized					
3. The content presented in the manual was useful to me as a faculty member					
4. I feel confident in using the tools and activities to support my reflective practice					
5. Tools and activities provided will enhance my reflective practice					
6. The content challenged my understanding of reflective practice					
7. I would recommend this manual to other faculty members					
8. Overall, I would rate this manual as:	Poor	Fair	Good	Very Good	Excellent

Are there other components that would have been helpful to include in this manual?

General comments and suggestions:

Thank you for taking the time to complete this evaluation.
Please e-mail colt@centennialcollege.ca **with your completed evaluation.**

References

Blaschke, L.M. (2012). Heutagogy and lifelong learning: A review of heutagogical practice and self-determined learning. *International Review of Research in Open and Distance Learning, 13*(1), http://www.irrodl.org/index.php/irrodl/article/view/1076/2113.

Boyer, E. (1990). *Scholarship Reconsidered: Priorities of the Professoriate*. San Francisco, CA: Jossey-Bass.

Brookfield, S. (2005). *The power of critical theory for adult learning and teaching*. Maidenhead, UK: Open University Press.

Brookfield, S.D. (1995). *Becoming a critically reflective teacher*. San Francisco, CA: Jossey-Bass.

Canfield, J., & Victor Hansen, M. (1996). *A 3rd Serving of Chicken Soup for the Soul*. Retrieved from: http://www.chickensoup.com/book/21729/a-3rd-serving-of-chicken-soup-for-the-soul.

Centennial College (2013). *Leading through Learning: Academic Plan 2013-2020*. https://www.centennialcollege.ca/pdf/publications/Academic-Plan.pdf

Center for New Designs in Teaching and Scholarship. (n.d.). Inclusive Pedagogy. Washington, DC: Georgetown University. https://cndls.georgetown.edu/inclusive-pedagogy/

Connolly, H., D'Hondt, J., Herie, M., & Selby, P. (2011). Adapting and developing educational best practices and curricula for Aboriginal tobacco cessation interventions, in White, J.P., Peters, J., Dinsdale, P. and Beavon D. *Aboriginal Policy Research: Health and Well-Being*, Volume IX. Toronto, ON: Thompson Educational Publishing.

Corneli, J., & Danoff, C.J. (2011). ParagogyPaper2, in Sebastian Hellmann, S, Frischmuth, P. Auer, S, and Dietrich, D (eds.), *Proceedings of the 6th Open Knowledge Conference*, Berlin, Germany, June 30 & July 1, 2011, http://ceur-ws.org/Vol-739/paper_5.pdf., http://paragogy.net/ParagogyPaper2.

Day, C. (1999). Researching teaching through reflective practice. In J. J. Loughran (Ed.), *Researching Teaching: Methodologies and Practices for Understanding Pedagogy*. London, UK: Falmer.

References

Freire, P. (2006, first English pub date 1970). *Pedagogy of the Oppressed, 30th Anniversary ed.* New York, NY: Continuum.

Frenk, J., Chen, L., Bhutta, Z.A., Cohen, J., Crisp, N., Evans, T., ... & Kistnasamy, B. (2010). Health professionals for a new century: transforming education to strengthen health systems in an interdependent world. *The Lancet, 376*(9756), 1923-1958.

Fullan, M. and Langworthy, M. (2013). *Towards a new end: New pedagogies for deep learning*. Seattle, WA: Collaborative Impact.

Fullan, M. and Langworthy, M. (2014). *A rich seam: How new pedagogies find deep learning*. London, UK: Pearson.

Grabove, V., Kustra, E., Lopes, V., Potter, M.K., Wiggers, R., & Woodhouse R. (2012). *Teaching and Learning Centres: Their evolving role within Ontario colleges and universities*. Toronto, ON: Higher Education Quality Council of Ontario (HEQCO). Retrieved from: http://www.heqco.ca/SiteCollectionDocuments/TL%20Centres%20ENG.pdf

Gruppen, L. D., Frohna, A. Z., Anderson, R. M., & Lowe, K. D. (2003). Faculty development for educational leadership and scholarship. *Academic Medicine, 78*(2), 137-141.

Hase, S., & Kenyon, C. (2000). From andragogy to heutagogy. *Ultibase Articles, 5*(3), 1-10.

Healey, M. (2000). Developing the scholarship of teaching in higher education: A discipline-based approach. *Higher Education Research and Development, 19*(2), 169-189.

Herie, M. (2005). Theoretical perspectives in online pedagogy. *Journal of Technology in Human Services, 23*(1-2), 29-52.

Herie, M. (2013). Andragogy 2.0? Teaching and Learning in the Global Classroom: Heutagogy and Paragogy. *Global Citizen Digest, 2*(2), 8-14.

hooks, b. (1994). *Teaching to Transgress. Education as the practice of freedom*. London, UK: Routledge.

Jay, J.K., & Johnson, K.L. (2002). Capturing complexity: A typology of reflective practice for teacher education. *Teaching and Teacher Education, 18*(1), 73-85.

Johnson, C., Williams, L., Parisi, J., & Brunkan, M. (2016). Behavioral characteristics and instructional patterns of expert teaching, and the transfer of those behaviors into a musical setting: Two case studies. *International Journal of Music Education, 34*(3), 299-310.

Kea, C.D., & Trent, S.C. (2013). Providing culturally responsive teaching in field-based and student teaching experiences: A case study. *Interdisciplinary Journal of Teaching and Learning, 3*(2), 82-101.

Kereluik, K., Mishra, P., Fahnoe, C., & Terry, L. (2013). What knowledge is of most worth: Teacher knowledge for 21st century learning. *Journal of Digital Learning in Teacher Education, 29*(4), 127-140.

Knowles, M.S. et al. (1984). *Andragogy in action: Applying modern principles of adult education*. San Francisco, CA: Jossey-Bass.

Larrivee, B. (2000). Transforming teaching practice: Becoming the critically reflective teacher. *Reflective Practice, 1*(3), 293-307.

Loughran, J.J. (2002). Effective reflective practice: In search of meaning in learning about teaching. *Journal of Teacher Education, 53*(1), 33-43.

Lueddeke, G.R. (2003). Professionalising teaching practice in higher education: A study of disciplinary variation and 'teaching-scholarship'. *Studies in Higher Education, 28*(2), 213-228.

Mann, K., Gordon, J., & MacLeod, A. (2009). Reflection and reflective practice in health professions education: a systematic review. *Advances in Health Sciences Education, 14*(4), 595-621.

McAlpine, I. (2000). Collaborative Learning Online. *Distance Education, 21*(1), 66-80.

Oliver, R. (1999). Exploring strategies for online teaching and learning. *Distance Education, 20*(2), 254.

References

Pozarnik, B.M., & Lavric, A. (2015). Fostering the quality of teaching and learning by developing the "neglected half" of university teachers' competencies. *Center for Educational Policy Studies Journal, 5*(2), 73-93.

Randall, N., Heaslip, P., & Morrison, D. (2013). Campus-based educational development & professional learning: Dimensions & directions. Vancouver, BC: BCcampus.

Richlin, L. (2001). Scholarly teaching and the scholarship of teaching. *New Directions for Teaching and Learning, 86*, 57-68.

Robles, J.R., Youmans, S.L., Byrd, D.C., & Polk, R.E. (2009). Perceived barriers to scholarship and research among pharmacy practice faculty: Survey report from the AACP scholarship/research faculty development task force. *American Journal of Pharmaceutical Education, 73*(1),1-11.

Ryerson University. (2012). Universal Design for Learning. Retrieved from: http://www.ryerson.ca/content/dam/lt/resources/instructionaldesign/UDLRecommendations.pdf

Schön, D.A. (1983). *The reflective practitioner: How professionals think in action*. London, UK: Temple Smith.

Schön, D.A. (1987). *Educating the reflective practitioner: Toward a new design for teaching and learning in the professions*. San Francisco, CA: Jossey-Bass.

Schön, D.A. (1992). *The reflective turn: Case studies in and on educational practice*. New York, NY: Teachers College Press.

Smyth, W.J. (1992). Teachers' work and the politics of reflection. *American Educational Research Journal, 29*(2), 267-300.

Tigelaar, D.E., Dolmans, D.H., Wolfhagen, I.H., & Van Der Vleuten, C.P. (2004). The development and validation of a framework for teaching competencies in higher education. *Higher Education, 48*(2), 253-268.

Tremmel, R. (1993). Zen and the art of reflective practice in teacher education. *Harvard Educational Review, 63*(4), 434-459.

Valli, L. (1992). *Reflective teacher education: Cases and critiques*. Albany, NY: State University of New York Press.

Van Der Werf, M., & Sabatier, G. (2009). *The college of 2020: Students*. North Hollywood, CA: Chronicle Research Services.

Wu, A. (2003). Supporting electronic discourse: Principles of design for a social constructivist perspective. *Journal of Interactive Learning Research*, *14*(2), 167-185.

Zeichner, K.M., & Liston, D.P. (1996). *Reflective teaching: An introduction*. Mahwah, NJ: Lawrence Erlbaum Associates.